THE SYRIAN HUMANITARIAN CRISIS: FOUR YEARS LATER AND NO END IN SIGHT

JOINT HEARING

BEFORE THE

SUBCOMMITTEE ON
THE MIDDLE EAST AND NORTH AFRICA

AND THE

SUBCOMMITTEE ON AFRICA, GLOBAL HEALTH, GLOBAL HUMAN RIGHTS, AND INTERNATIONAL ORGANIZATIONS

OF THE

COMMITTEE ON FOREIGN AFFAIRS
HOUSE OF REPRESENTATIVES

ONE HUNDRED FOURTEENTH CONGRESS

FIRST SESSION

FEBRUARY 12, 2015

Serial No. 114–7

Printed for the use of the Committee on Foreign Affairs

Available via the World Wide Web: http://www.foreignaffairs.house.gov/ or http://www.gpo.gov/fdsys/

U.S. GOVERNMENT PUBLISHING OFFICE

93–286PDF   WASHINGTON : 2015

For sale by the Superintendent of Documents, U.S. Government Publishing Office
Internet: bookstore.gpo.gov   Phone: toll free (866) 512–1800; DC area (202) 512–1800
Fax: (202) 512–2104   Mail: Stop IDCC, Washington, DC 20402–0001

CONTENTS

THE SYRIAN HUMANITARIAN CRISIS: FOUR YEARS LATER AND NO END IN SIGHT

THURSDAY, FEBRUARY 12, 2015

House of Representatives,
Subcommittee on the Middle East and North Africa and
Subcommittee on Africa, Global Health,
Committee on Foreign Affairs,
Washington, DC.

The committees met, pursuant to notice, at 1:30 p.m., in room 2172 Rayburn House Office Building, Hon. Ileana Ros-Lehtinen (chairman of the Subcommittee on Middle East and North Africa) presiding.

Ms. Ros-Lehtinen. With all due apologies to the members who are not here yet, I am going to start because pretty soon we will be going back into the session and be voting. So, thank you very much. I know that the members will be coming right quick. When they come here, I will recognize them for their opening statements.

So, the joint subcommittees will come to order.

After recognizing myself, Chairman Smith, Ranking Members Deutch and Bass, as soon as they come for 5 minutes each for our opening statements, I will, then, recognize any other members seeking recognition for 1 minute. We will, then, hear from our witnesses.

Without objection, the witnesses' prepared statements will be made a part of the record, and members may have 5 days in which to insert statements and questions for the record, subject to the length limitation in the rules.

Before I begin my opening remarks, I want to take a moment to offer our most sincere condolences to the friends and family of Kayla Mueller. Our thoughts and prayers are with them in this most trying of times. Kayla was taken hostage while doing humanitarian work in Syria, which is the subject of our hearing, helping those who are in such dire need of her help. All of America mourns her loss and the family's loss.

The terrorists have proven time and again that they have no respect for human rights, and that is why we must redouble our efforts to defeat this scourge and its radical ideology. Kayla's legacy will be the work that she had done to alleviate the suffering of a countless many in Syria and around the world.

It is important that our Government will continue to respond to this humanitarian crisis, but also that we will make the respect for human rights across the globe a priority and not just an afterthought.

With that, the Chair now recognizes herself for 5 minutes.

Next month will mark the fourth anniversary since the start of the Syrian conflict, and there are no signs that the crisis will abate anytime soon. Assad has demonstrated no remorse, and, indeed, his intransigence has only hardened as he maintains his grasp on power and the enclaves of Syria, thanks to the support from Iran and the United States' unwillingness to engage both ISIL and Assad in a comprehensive strategy. ISIL and other terror groups have managed to wrest control of other large areas of Syria, and they, too, have no intention of giving up the territory they have claimed.

Since President Obama announced strikes against Syria last September, ISIL has actually gained more territory. That leaves little territory for those Syrians who wish to flee the fighting and flee the violence. What we are seeing unfold in Syria is one of the worst humanitarian crises in the region in recent memory, and it isn't just limited to Syrian and Iraq. Jordan and other neighboring countries have been forced to bear the brunt of a massive influx of refugees fleeing the fighting. That has tested the limits of their already-strained capabilities.

Last Congress Ranking Member Ted Deutch and I convened four hearings on the humanitarian situation in Syria. One we were pleased to join with Congressman Smith's and Congresswoman Bass' subcommittee in an effort to continue to shine a light on this aspect of the conflict that gets ignored.

When we held our first subcommittee hearing on the situation Syria, 80,000 Syrians has been killed and 1.5 million people had been displaced. Less than 2 years later, those numbers have swelled. Over 200,000 have been killed, more than 3 million have fled, and now more than half of Syria's population is in dire need of humanitarian assistance.

The U.S. has been the largest provider of humanitarian assistance in response to the crisis, providing much-needed aid to Syria, to Iraq, to Jordan, and other countries that have been severely impacted by this crisis. We have spent over $3 billion since the start of the conflict, and the President's budget request, released last week, is seeking an additional $1.6 billion to address the humanitarian needs in Syria and in Iraq.

While some of this goes directly to the neighboring countries that host refugees and directly to the NGOs, the vast majority of our funding for Syria supports multilateral initiatives through the United States. I worry that some of the assistance we provide that goes to the U.N. and its implementing partners might get diverted to ISIL or other terrorist groups or the Assad regime by force or through bribes, in order to gain access to certain areas.

While I understand there are some very real and dangerous obstacles in place to reaching the maximum amount of people, Americans are concerned over where this $5 billion is going, especially if most of it could be going through third and fourth parties, as evidence shows that it is.

There have been reports that some of the humanitarian assistance is going through middlemen in Syrian when the implementing partners can't get access to the locations that they are trying to reach. More recently, food rations have been handed out by the

World Food Program, and they are tagged with the Islamic State symbol.

So, there are some very real and pressing problems that need to be corrected. Congress and the administration, we have a responsibility to the American public to be good stewards of their tax dollars. So, it is imperative that we find the right balance of efficiency and transparency. Our comprehensive strategy toward Syria must take into effect the humanitarian crisis that we are confronting today.

That is why it is so important, it is imperative, that we hold these hearings not only to hear from the vital work that we are doing and the lives that we are saving, but also conduct our proper oversight role. It is also why I was joined this week by Ranking Member Deutch, Mr. DeSantis, and Mr. Connolly in sending a request to the Government Accountability Office, GAO, requesting a report to ensure that our aid is reaching its intended recipients and to get a better understanding regarding our visibility into the large sums of money that we send through the U.N.

The Syrian humanitarian crisis is not a problem that is going away anytime soon, not until we defeat ISIL and Assad, and Assad is removed from power. But the U.S. cannot afford to continue to provide billions indefinitely. It is imperative that we have confidence that what we are providing is not subject to waste, fraud, abuse, or diversion to terror groups, so that we can continue playing a key role in responding to this crisis and maximize our effectiveness.

With that, I am proud to yield to the ranking member of our subcommittee, Mr. Deutch.

Mr. DEUTCH. Thank you, Madam Chairman.

I, too, would like to associate myself with the chairman's remarks about the tragic death of Kayla Mueller at the hands of the barbaric ISIS terrorists. Our thoughts and prayers go out to Kayla's family and friends during this difficult time. Please know that we will continue to honor Kayla's memory and her life's work by giving this humanitarian crisis the attention that it deserves.

I want to thank the chairman for starting this Congress with a hearing specifically focused on the humanitarian aspect of the Syrian conflict, a followup to four humanitarian-focused hearings that we held last Congress.

The title of this hearing speaks volumes to the situation inside Syria and in neighboring countries. There is no end in sight. Members had the opportunity to discuss the political and security components of this conflict in the full Foreign Affairs Committee this morning, but this afternoon we are here to focus on the growing humanitarian crisis.

There are now 2.2 million people in need of humanitarian assistance. As Mr. Staal's testimony notes, that is the populations of New York City and Los Angeles, the two largest cities in the United States combined. There are 3.8 million refugees in neighboring countries. There are 241,000 people in besieged areas inside Syria. There are 9.8 million people who are food insecure. Madam Chairman, these numbers are truly staggering.

The situation inside Syria has complicated the ability of humanitarian organizations to effectively deliver aid. Despite the first authorization of cross-border aid deliveries in the United Nations Security Council Resolution 2165, it is becoming increasingly difficult to get aid safely into the country and to its intended recipients.

Deputy Assistant Secretary Clements, I hope you will speak to the effectiveness of cross-border and cross-line aid. We continue to engage in a political process that is yet to even yield a sustainable truce inside Syria, an effort that would at least help deliver aid to those with the most critical needs.

Syrian refugees have flooded into Jordan, Lebanon, and Turkey at a staggering rate. Jordan has 622,000 registered refugees, and in Lebanon the Syrian refugees now make up one-fourth of the population. These overwhelming numbers do not even include potentially hundreds of thousands of unregistered refugees that have been absorbed into urban areas. We have got to continue to support these host communities and help to mitigate the understandable strain that it places on their resources.

The United States has now provided over $3.5 billion in humanitarian assistance. We are the largest individual donor. I offer my full support of continued humanitarian funding for this crisis, but I also want to make sure that our aid is effective and not falling into the wrong hands.

I was troubled by reports last week that showed ISIS fighters handing out U.N. food packages. That is why, as Chairman Ros-Lehtinen had mentioned, I joined with her and Congressmen Connolly and DeSantis in commissioning a GAO report, so we can be absolutely sure that the proper mechanisms are in place to spend our aid dollars most effectively.

I have got to say I have been shocked and truly dismayed throughout this crisis at the lack of financial support coming from the international community. Last year only half of the U.N. budget was funded. These unfulfilled pledges of assistance led to the World Food Program literally having to stop its operations while an emergency fundraising campaign took place. That is unacceptable.

I recognize that most of us were unprepared to deal with a protracted crisis. Now, after 4 years, we are at risk of losing an entire generation; 5.6 million children have been affected.

We have seen the outbreak of formerly eradicated diseases like polio, simply because infants and children couldn't get vaccinations. Refugee children have been absorbed into unfamiliar school systems, many of which didn't have the staff or resources necessary to shoulder these additional students. Many have been forced to abandon school altogether and find work to help support their families.

Women and children have borne the brunt of this humanitarian crisis. I hope that Mr. Staal can address some of the programs that we are funding aimed at protecting these vulnerable populations.

Before I close, I want to remind everyone of one critical factor. Despite the horrific brutality of ISIS and its devastating attacks in Syria and Iraq and against American and other Western citizens, it is still the ruthless Assad regime that remains the biggest threat to the Syrian people. We may share a common enemy in ISIS, but we are not partners with this deadly regime that has the blood of hundreds of thousands of its own people on its hands.

Finally, I want to commend the work of State and USAID. This is a tremendous challenge, and we recognize the work you do is not easy. The work of your partners on the ground who risk their lives to help those in need deserves to be recognized in this body and in capitals around the world every day.

I thank our witnesses for being here.

Ms. ROS-LEHTINEN. Very good. Thank you, Mr. Deutch.

I am so pleased to yield to the subcommittee chairman, Chairman Smith, who has made it his life's mission to fight human rights violations and to spearhead humanitarian missions. Thank you, Mr. Chairman.

Mr. SMITH. Madam Chair, thank you so very much. It is an honor and a privilege to join you, for both of our subcommittees to be receiving this testimony and really broadcasting to all who will hear our solidarity with the victims, those men, women, and children who are being savagely beaten and killed and raped and tortured by Assad and by other players and other actors in Syria. So, thank you again for pulling us together for this hearing.

As we all know, since the beginning of the Syrian conflict in 2011, the U.N. estimates that more than 200,000 have been killed. It would be terrible enough if we could count the dead in Syria as collateral damage from a civil war gone completely out of control. Unfortunately, the truth is far more horrific than that.

According to the U.N., the government of Bashar al-Assad initiated the conflict to crush the opposition to his brutal rule. In the process, he has used chemical weapons, barrel bombs, and other weapons of mass destruction to kill his own people. This regime has been involved in widespread killings, including children, torture, again, against children, as well as hospital patients, arbitrary arrests and imprisonment on a massive scale, deployment of tanks and helicopter gunships in densely-populated areas, heavy and indiscriminate shelling of civilian areas, enforced disappearances, systematic destruction of property and looting, systematic denial of food and water in some areas, and prevention of medical treatment, again, including children. So depraved has the Assad regime been, that it has been reported to have indiscriminately shelled bakeries with artillery rounds, even though the targets were civilian, and not military, targets.

David Nott, a British volunteer surgeon in Syria, reported in 2013 that ''Victims of government snipers would display wounds in a particular area of the body on particular days,'' indicating that they may have been targeted in a gruesome game.

The Syrian Government came to view doctors and nurses as collaborators because they were willing to help rebels in need of medical care. Early on in the conflict, the Assad regime imprisoned hundreds of health workers and tortured many of them to death. Others have just disappeared. Government forces targeted health workers in medical facilities in attacks, erasing the universal principle of medical neutrality.

However, the government isn't the only perpetrator of human rights violations in Syria. The U.N. reports that armed opposition groups, including militia supporting the Assad regime, have been responsible for unlawful and indiscriminate killings, tortured abuse, including hostage-taking. One rebel commander told the Associated Press that his group had released prisoners in bomb-rigged cars, turning them into unwitting suicide bombers. Other groups have perpetrated crimes too egregious to present today in detail.

In addition to armed groups such as the Free Syrian Army and the Syrian Revolutionaries Front, al-Qaeda and its offshoot, including al-Nusra Front, ISIS, operate within this conflict committing heinous crimes against those unable to leave Syria.

We know—and this was in the testimony by the Deputy Assistant Secretary Clements—half of its prewar population in Syria has been displaced. Half of a country gone, displaced, and that is almost without precedent anywhere in the world.

The Euro-Mediterranean Human Rights Network reported in late 2013 that at least 6,000 women have been reported being raped by one armed group or another, and that the genuine figure was likely much higher due to underreporting. In fact, the International Rescue Committee reported 2 years ago that the primary reason for Syrians to flee their country has been fear of rape.

The various armed groups terrorizing people in Syria operate with impunity. Since Syria is not a party to the Rome Statute, the International Criminal Court has no jurisdiction over these human rights violators, although there could be a referral, if they were so inclined, from the Security Council. Even if the ICC could get involved, Russia has already indicated its opposition to that kind of referral.

That is why again I introduced last year—and I will do it again soon—a resolution to create an independent tribunal to begin the process of investigating human rights crimes in Syria and bring to reality the promise of justice to those who now have no fear of any kind of accountability. It would be patterned on what we had in Yugoslavia, Rwanda, and, of course, the Independent Court in Sierra Leone.

The tribunal would prosecute the perpetrators of mass atrocities, war crimes, and crimes against humanity, no matter who committed the crime. Hopefully, these individuals would be brought to justice.

Again, I want to thank you, Madam Chair, for doing this hearing together with our subcommittees and for your extraordinary leadership.

Ms. ROS-LEHTINEN. Thank you so much, a powerful statement.

Because Ms. Bass, the ranking member of Mr. Smith's committee, is not here, I would like to recognize Ms. Frankel and Mr. Boyle to share those 5 minutes, however way you would like to divide them.

Ms. Frankel is recognized.

Ms. FRANKEL. Thank you, Madam Chair. I thank both you and the ranking member for this hearing, which I believe is very important.

I want to share your sentiments on or sorrow for the loss of Kayla Mueller.

We have heard from the administration, obviously, in the past several months why we should train and arm Syrian rebels. We now have a request for authorization for the use of military force.

So, I am very pleased that you are here to talk about—it is a little change of pace; let's put it that way.

This is what I am particularly interested in, not only the type of humanitarian assistance and answering some of the questions about whether we are effectively getting it to those who are suffering, but I am also interested in your opinion as to the role that humanitarian assistance in the larger goal of defeating those forces like Assad, like ISIL, that are causing the pain.

Then, what else I would be interested in, especially in light of what happened to Kayla Mueller, is how safe it is for our AID workers in delivering this humanitarian assistance.

I thank you, and I will yield the rest of my time to Mr. Boyle.

Ms. ROS-LEHTINEN. Mr. Boyle is recognized.

Mr. BOYLE. Thank you very much.

I have to say, being on the Foreign Affairs Committee and this subcommittee for the last 6 weeks, I keep waiting until we get to have hearings about good news. I suspect that we would be waiting a very long time.

The scale of the human tragedy that has taken place in Syria is unbelievable, now over 12 million human beings, 12 million people, who have been dislocated. This has created enormous instability not just in Syria, but, obviously, in northern Iraq and in other nearby areas.

I would just ask—and a lot of my comments were echoed earlier—so, rather than being repetitive, I would just ask that, when you are giving your statements, while this subject might be specifically about Syria, this is part of a regional fight, part of a fight that King Hussein of Jordan said has been going on for approximately 1,400 years, I would like you to talk about, to the extent that you are knowledgeable about it, the stability of the regime in Jordan. Because with being bordered with Israel and what was going on last summer in Gaza and the disruptions to a lesser extent in the West Bank, and then, of course, what is going on, a de facto Shia-Sunni civil war, and, also, at the same time a war between those who believe in a very radical militant, violent form of Islam and those who do not, with all that going in the region, we have one little island of stability smack dab in the middle there. I am deeply concerned, and you do not hear about this much, but I am deeply concerned that the Syrian conflict, if it were to spread to the West, would finally topple one of the few regimes that we can actually count on as an ally. So, I hope that when you give your comments, you will broaden it and talk about that a bit.

I thank the Madam Chair. It is an honor to be on her subcommittee. I thank the ranking member.

Also, to say this in person, I have watched the human rights work that Chairman Smith has done for many, many years, and am a big admirer of it. It is great to be a part of this.

Ms. ROS-LEHTINEN. It is an honor to have you. Thank you very much.

Mr. Chabot of Ohio.

Mr. CHABOT. Thank you, Madam Chairman, for calling this important joint hearing.

The violence in Syria over the past 4 years has spiraled out of control, as we know, yielding a serious and grave humanitarian crisis. It was in August 2012 that the President famously declared the red line. However, today nearly 200,000 people have been senselessly killed, over 3 million are refugees in neighboring countries, with millions more internally displaced, and we are no closer to ending this humanitarian tragedy.

As this work continues, I believe that this crisis will, unfortunately, only get worse. The refugee flows into Jordan, Lebanon, and Turkey have hardly diminished, and these countries are at their peak in terms of the numbers that they can support. At the same time, unprecedented numbers are streaming into Syria to join ISIL and other extremist groups, which are further complicating and exacerbating this situation.

As the U.S. is the largest contributor of humanitarian assistance, we need to implement a strategy that most effectively deals with this growing crisis, while ensuring those in most need are receiving our support. Various reports have indicated that U.S. assistance is reaching the hands of ISIS and other terrorist groups, and that is very alarming.

I hope that today's witnesses will discuss what is being done to address this issue and all the other things my colleagues have mentioned. There is, indeed, a lot to talk about today.

Thank you, Madam Chair, and I yield back the balance.

Ms. ROS-LEHTINEN. Thank you, Mr. Chabot.

Mr. Trott is recognized. Dr. Yoho is recognized.

Mr. YOHO. Thank you, Madam Chair. I just want to say I look forward to hearing your information, so that we can come to some common-sense solutions to the Middle East over there and work with the AUMF and the President to get some resolution.

With that, I yield back.

Ms. ROS-LEHTINEN. Thank you very much.

So now, we turn to our witnesses. Let me introduce our panelists.

First, we are pleased to welcome Deputy Assistant Secretary Kelly Clements of the Bureau of Population, Refugees, and Migration at the Department of State. She was detailed to the Office of the U.N. High Commissioner of Refugees in Bangladesh and has served on the State Department's Task Force on Kurdish Refugees and Displaced Persons. She has also been a Special Assistant to the Under Secretary of State for Global Affairs and a Senior Emergency Office for Europe during the Balkan crisis.

Welcome.

Then, we will also hear from Acting Assistant Administrator Thomas Staal of the Bureau of Democracy, Conflict, and Humanitarian Assistance at USAID. He has served in USAID since the late eighties and has managed project developments in eastern and southern Africa as well as in the West Bank and Gaza. More recently, he has served as the Director of the Iraq Reconstruction Office here in Washington, DC, and as Mission Director in Lebanon, Ethiopia, and Iraq.

Excellent panelists.

We will begin with you, Ms. Clements.

The prepared statements will be made a part of the record.

STATEMENT OF MS. KELLY TALLMAN CLEMENTS, DEPUTY AS-SISTANT SECRETARY, BUREAU OF POPULATION, REFUGEES, AND MIGRATION, U.S. DEPARTMENT OF STATE

Ms. CLEMENTS. Thank you so much, Chairman Ros-Lehtinen, Ranking Member Deutch, Chairman Smith, and members of the committee, for inviting us to this very important hearing on humanitarian assistance for those imperiled and uprooted by the worst human-made catastrophe of our time.

I have submitted my full testimony for the record, and I am grateful for the opportunity to update you and to thank you for your leadership and to Congress for its unwavering support.

The Syrian crisis has claimed nearly 200,000 lives, forcibly displaced half of Syria's prewar population of 24 million people. Almost 4 million have fled to neighboring countries and many will remain in exile for years to come.

The Assad regime and extremist groups target innocent civilians already suffering from food shortages, inadequate shelter, and preventable diseases. Right now, 12.2 million people inside Syria need urgent humanitarian aid, and half of them are children.

The humanitarian response has been the most expensive in modern history, and the needs have outstripped available resources. Although U.N. humanitarian appeals have grown exponentially, the total amount pledged has plateaued. The 2014 appeals were just over half-funded, as you noted earlier.

The United States remains the single largest donor and has contributed over $3 billion since the crisis began. In 2014, my Bureau at the State Department provided more than a third of all funding for the Syrian humanitarian response. That $725 million is the largest single-year contribution in our Bureau's history. Roughly half of all U.S. humanitarian aid has gone to conflict victims inside Syria and half to refugees and communities hosting them.

Over the last 6 months, U.N. Security Council Resolutions 2191, 2139, 2165 enabled U.N. convoys to cross borders and battle lines and to reach millions of civilians in governorates, including Dar'a, Idlib, Quneitra, and Aleppo that have been encircled, blockaded, and under siege.

In 2014, the U.N. Refugee Agency provided aid to more than one out of every three Syrians in need, including 1 million people in difficult-to-reach areas. USAID feeds nearly half of all Syrian refugees, roughly 2 million people, and provides relief items, everything from cooking pots to shoes and blankets to insulated tents to help refugee families survive the winter. Our programs aid survivors of gender-based violence, elderly and disabled people, unaccompanied children, and others who need services and protection. With U.S. support, in 2014, the U.N. and its strong NGO partners were able to triple the number of Syrian children enrolled in school.

But vast needs remain. Half of Syrian children are still not in school. Last week Tom Staal and I saw thousands of them while visiting the Domiz Camp in the Iraqi Kurdistan region. It is bursting at the seams with an official tally of 35,000, but far more are seeking services not available in overwhelmed host communities.

Heroic efforts are underway to educate, feed, shelter, and clothe the displaced, but everything is in short supply. More than eight in ten Syrian refugees live outside of camps, straining host communities across a region that was already economically fragile and politically volatile. Syrian refugees are crowded into communities in Turkey, Lebanon, Jordan, Iraq, and Egypt. In Lebanon, one in four residents is now a refugee. In Jordan, housing shortages have doubled rents; schools and hospitals are overcrowded; municipal services cannot keep up; tensions are rising, and beleaguered governments have responded by closing or tightly managing borders.

To ease these pressures, the Department and USAID are coordinating humanitarian and development assistance and funding projects that provide important services, clean water, sanitization, education, and economic opportunities to both host communities and refugees.

We have encouraged other donors to come forward, and many have been generous, including Saudi Arabia and Kuwait. The United States is also accelerating resettlement of Syrian refugees. We have received referrals from over 10,000 Syrian refugees and expect to admit between 1,000 and 2,000 this fiscal year and many more in 2016 and beyond.

Thank you very much for your support, and I welcome your questions.

[The prepared statement of Ms. Clements follows:]

**Testimony of Deputy Assistant Secretary Kelly T. Clements
Before the House Foreign Affairs Subcommittee on the Middle East and
North Africa and the Subcommittee on Africa, Global Health, Global Human
Rights, and International Organizations**

"The Syrian Humanitarian Crisis: Four Years Later and No End in Sight"

February 12, 2015

Chairwoman Ros-Lehtinen, Chairman Smith and Members of the Committee, thank you for inviting us to this important hearing on humanitarian assistance for those imperiled and uprooted by the violence in Syria. I am grateful for the opportunity to update you on how the U.S. government is targeting life-saving aid, on the impact of our efforts, and on the challenges ahead.

I would also like to thank you for your leadership and Congress for its generous and unwavering support for the humanitarian response we have been undertaking in Syria and in the region. U.S. leadership and resources are playing an essential role, enabling us and the organizations we fund to cope with emergencies and protracted, complex crises, to ease suffering and save innocent lives.

Historic High in Simultaneous Global Emergencies

It is hard to think of a time when the need has been greater. Not since World War II raged across three continents has violence and persecution driven so many people from their homes. Right now, there are over 50 million refugees, asylum seekers, and internally displaced persons in the world. In addition to the cataclysm in Syria, we face major crises in Iraq, the Central African Republic, South Sudan, Gaza, Ukraine, Somalia, and Yemen. As these crises fester and convulse many nations, they are stretching the international community's ability to respond.

With limited resources, our strategy has been to provide the basics in order to keep people alive—and making sure that we find and assist the most vulnerable among them. Many things that we regard as basic rights, like children going to school or women delivering their babies in clean, safe places, have become luxuries, and would not be possible for many without the presence of international humanitarian actors. Collectively, we are saving lives. The United States has been the leader in providing this assistance. To date, thanks to support from Congress, we have contributed over $3 billion in assistance to Syria and the region.

In 2014, the level of global humanitarian assistance rose to a record $22 billion. But even this enormous amount is not enough to provide basic life-saving relief to all of those most in need. This is certainly true in the case of Syria. The Syrian crisis is the worst human-made catastrophe of our time, requiring one of the most expensive humanitarian responses in history. UN humanitarian appeals have grown exponentially over the last three years, and the total amount given by donors has remained roughly the same. The 2014 appeals for assistance inside Syria and for refugees in surrounding countries were just over half funded. This year's estimate of what will be needed climbed higher still. The UN's recently launched 2015 appeals for response to the Syria crisis exceed $8 billion.

Funding shortages have hindered the response and left critical needs unmet. Tom and I just returned from Iraq a few days ago, and while we were there we visited refugees and IDPs alike with government authorities and aid agencies struggling to respond to enormous humanitarian needs. Domiz Camp in the Iraqi Kurdistan Region is bursting at the seams with an official tally of 35,000, but far more seeking services not available in overwhelmed host communities. Camps are under construction, but not available fast enough to house one of the most dynamic population movements in modern history. Heroic efforts are underway to educate, feed, shelter, and clothe the displaced, but there are not enough openings in schools or latrines for families to take care of basic needs. We saw firsthand how the lack of funding has hampered relief efforts. To deliver healthcare, mobile clinics have become static clinics in order to handle the demand for medical services in the camp. At child friendly centers we saw thousands of children who have missed critical years of primary education, but remained upbeat, grateful for the chance to learn and resume their normal lives. Unless we get more of them in school, they risk becoming a "lost generation."

Syria's Dismal Milestones
So far, the conflict has claimed the lives of over 200,000 Syrians. According to the UN Commission of Inquiry, most of them died at the hands of the Syrian regime. The Syrian crisis has set unenviable records, producing almost four million refugees, more than any other modern conflict, and forcibly displacing more than seven million internally, the vast majority as a result of the Assad regime's campaign of destruction. Cumulatively, half of its pre-war population has been displaced. Many of the refugees who have fled the country are unable or unwilling to return to Syria anytime soon. In a few short years, Syria has been transformed from a middle income country that hosted hundreds of thousands of

refugees from Iraq and elsewhere into the largest refugee-producing country in the world.

Inside Syria, the Assad regime and extremist groups continue to target innocent civilians, who are already suffering from sieges, food shortages, inadequate shelter, and what used to be preventable diseases.

Addressing Iraq in the Syria Context

The crisis has wreaked havoc beyond Syria's borders, incubating violent extremism and the rise of the Islamic State in Iraq and the Levant (ISIL) in both Syria and Iraq. ISIL's attacks and reign of terror have displaced millions of Iraqis and Syrians. It is important to note though, that the political situations in Syria and Iraq differ. In Iraq, we have a strong partner in the Iraqi government. In Syria, the regime remains the single largest threat to the Syrian people.

We recognize that the challenges are regional and integrated, and our humanitarian responses must be as well. There are many pieces to this complex puzzle. We are fitting them together, working hand in hand with our colleagues at USAID to ensure that we are thinking strategically, and aligning our Syria and Iraq responses to meet the emergency and protracted needs of conflict victims, refugees, and overstretched host communities. Along with USAID, we recognize that the nature of the crisis makes coordinating humanitarian and development assistance essential.

Quantifying What U.S. Humanitarian Assistance Has Done

Thanks to the U.S. Congress, the United States remains the single largest donor to the humanitarian response for Syria, contributing over $3.1 billion since the crisis began—in 2014 our contributions represented more than one-third of all funding to the crisis. Roughly half of our assistance has gone to conflict victims inside Syria, and half has gone to refugees and communities in the region that host them.

Since 2011, the Bureau of Population, Refugees, and Migration (PRM) has provided nearly $1.4 billion of this humanitarian aid. Last year alone, PRM's support for conflict-affected Syrians reached nearly $725 million, the largest single-year contribution to a humanitarian crisis in the history of the Bureau.

The results of that coordination and our assistance strategy are clear. The assistance we provide is saving lives both inside and outside Syria. Over the last six months we have overcome hurdles and aid has reached millions of civilians in dire need. By adopting UN Security Council Resolution 2191 and its predecessors, UNSCRs 2139 and 2165, the UN Security Council has authorized the UN to reach areas that were previously cut off from outside aid through the end of 2015. Aid has crossed international borders and conflict lines to reach civilians in Dar'a, Idlib, Quneitra and Aleppo governorates. UN convoys have crossed Syria's borders bringing food, water, winter relief items and medical supplies to 20% of conflict victims inside Syria since July 2014. The UN is also delivering aid *across conflict lines* inside Syria, getting into an average of 66 hard-to-access areas each month out of a total of 287. In 2014, with support from the United States and other donor governments, the UN High Commissioner for Refugees (UNHCR) provided aid to more than one out of every three Syrians in need, including nearly one million people who have been cut off in difficult-to-reach areas. UNHCR remains the Bureau's largest partner, but other aid organizations we fund have also provided much-needed relief supplies such as clean water, food and medicines to numbers close to half of Syrians in need.

American funded protection and assistance also supports refugees from Syria living in neighboring countries. In these countries, eighty-five percent of Syrian refugees live outside of camps, many housed in sub-standard shelter in urban settings. In 2014, aid agencies we fund helped improve shelter for over 20% of all Syrian refugees living in and outside camps. This included providing winter-proofed tents to help people in substandard and dangerous dwellings. They also provided access to safe drinking water for over one million refugees.

At least half of all refugee children from Syria are still not enrolled in school. In urban areas of Turkey, where the vast majority of 1.6 million refugees from Syria live, UNICEF cites enrollment rates below 20% in urban areas despite recent efforts by the Government to improve access to public schools. While schooling remains a challenge, with increasing numbers of refugee children and insufficient schooling options, we are making progress. With U.S. support, the UN and its NGO partners helped over 360,000 refugee children in neighboring countries enroll in school in 2014, triple the number enrolled in 2013.

The assistance the United States provides feeds nearly half of all Syrian refugees. Over 20% of all refugees received additional items to help them survive—from cooking pots to jerry cans for water to winter clothes and shoes. Over 75% of all Syrian refugees also received healthcare consultations and nearly 366,000 were referred to more specialized healthcare services for serious conditions or injuries.

Our programs also provide critical support for survivors of sexual and gender-based violence, mental health counseling services, assistance for the disabled and the elderly, and protection for unaccompanied minors.

Challenges

The crisis is placing enormous pressure on a region that was already economically fragile and politically volatile. As I mentioned earlier, Lebanon, Jordan, Turkey, Iraq, and Egypt are hosting nearly four million Syrian refugees. In Lebanon, one in four residents is now a refugee from Syria. In Jordan, housing is in such short supply that rents have doubled in some areas. In Lebanon and Jordan, schools are running double shifts, hospitals are overcrowded, and municipal services cannot keep up. Across the region, host community tensions have risen as Syrians work informally for lower wages in fields and factories in order to provide the most basic support for their families. Economic growth has slowed in communities that were already poor, exacerbating social tensions between host communities and Syrians. These types of tensions affect both refugees and communities hosting them, and impact the ability of communities to continue hosting refugees; thus our assistance must address the needs of both populations.

As hosting countries see no end in sight to this crisis, we have seen borders start to close. Lebanon and Jordan have joined Egypt in placing restrictions on Syrian arrivals. Turkey generously admitted nearly 200,000 mostly Kurdish Syrians that fled from ISIL's advance on Kobane in September and Iraq has also accepted over 25,000 Kurdish Syrians from the same influx, but these options may not be available for future waves of people in trouble. Refugees from Syria are running out of safe places to flee. In desperation, tens of thousands of Syrians are attempting dangerous boat journeys to reach asylum in Europe with diminishing options in the region.

U.S. diplomats have asked neighboring countries to keep their borders open and aid those in harm's way but in order to do so, they will need more help. We are redoubling efforts to get more aid to Syrians still inside Syria so that people are not forced to flee because they lack material goods. Neighboring countries deserve our steadfast support to help cope with refugee populations that will likely remain for many years to come. As part of that effort, the State Department is assisting communities hosting large populations of refugees. In Lebanon, our assistance has improved municipal services through rehabilitation of water systems, schools, and health clinics, which will last beyond the conflict to support host communities, but the needs remain great.

We also are working to integrate relief efforts with USAID's long-term development programs. Our joint efforts have provided hundreds of millions of dollars to projects that provide vital services, clean water, sanitation, education, and economic opportunities to both host communities and refugees. Meeting refugee needs in this way is new for us, but we see this as an important component of our effort to work with governments to keep borders open to vulnerable Syrians and ensuring their protection. It is much easier to aid people in need in the neighboring countries than in Syria. Fortunately, this crisis has also been an impetus to implement innovative and cost-effective ways to reach more people in need – for example by the use of debit cards, cash transfers, biometrics, and GPS tracking devices and barcode scanners for aid convoys to conflict areas.

Next Steps

Unmet needs and real risks loom ahead. Inside Syria, 2.9 million children require lifesaving vaccinations; 6.2 million people need monthly food rations; and 3.5 million children and adolescents should go to school. A failure to act could endanger millions of innocent civilians caught between the Syrian government and armed groups. Strong, sustained support from a larger donor base for the humanitarian response is critical and U.S. leadership remains essential.

As we plan our assistance for 2015, we also continue to urge other donors to increase their contributions to UN-led relief efforts. Donors have already been generous. The European Commission, Kuwait, Saudi Arabia, United Kingdom, Germany, Canada, Japan, Qatar and UAE have made significant contributions to UN-led relief operations for both Syrians and Iraqis.

We applaud, for instance, the tremendous generosity of Saudi Arabia, whose $500 million contribution to the UN in the early stages of the Iraq crisis last year helped many Iraqis affected by ISIL's violence. Saudi Arabia also stepped in with a $52 million contribution at the end of 2014 to the World Food Program when it exhausted their funding and faced the prospect of suspending food assistance to almost half of the region's Syrian refugees – two million people. Kuwait, for its part, has emerged as a regional leader on humanitarian issues. They have not only hosted two Ministerial-level pledging conferences — and plan to host the next conference on March 31 — they have also given $800 million to provide desperately needed food, shelter, and medical supplies. The March 31st pledging conference is an important opportunity for other countries to stand up and pledge their support for Syrians. In the past years, senior level U.S. bilateral engagement has been instrumental in encouraging non-traditional donors to step forward. We are working to encourage strong representation from an expanded pool of donors and ensure that we are sharing responsibility for the humanitarian response with the entire region and the entire community of nations. A top donors group mechanism also galvanizes support from Gulf states and keeps the spotlight on the Syrian crisis.

We and others have also stepped forward to resettle Syrian refugees. In recent months, the United States has received referrals for over 10,000 Syrian refugees. We're working with the Department of Homeland Security to interview and process these referrals, and expect to admit 1,000-2,000 in FY 2015, and higher numbers in FY 2016 and beyond. More Syrian refugees have arrived in the United States in this fiscal year than arrived in the last four years combined. With this refugee crisis threatening to become protracted, the U.S. resettlement program is another way for us to follow through on our commitment to extend help and hope to those displaced and endangered by the violence in Syria.

Thank you for your support and I welcome your questions.

Ms. ROS-LEHTINEN. Thank you very much, Ms. Clements. Mr. Staal?

STATEMENT OF MR. THOMAS STAAL, ACTING ASSISTANT ADMINISTRATOR, BUREAU FOR DEMOCRACY, CONFLICT AND HUMANITARIAN ASSISTANCE, U.S. AGENCY FOR INTERNATIONAL DEVELOPMENT

Mr. STAAL. Chairman Ros-Lehtinen, Ranking Member Deutch, Chairman Smith, and members of the subcommittees, thank you for the opportunity to testify today and for highlighting the needs of the Syrian people and the needs of the people in their neighborhood. For me, it is especially important because I grew up in the area and I have lived and worked there for many years.

As Deputy Assistant Secretary Clements has mentioned, and many of you know, the Syrian crisis is the largest and most complex humanitarian emergency of our time. More than 2.2 million Syrians are in need of humanitarian assistance. You mentioned New York and Los Angeles. It is also just about the entire population of the State of Pennsylvania, is another way to look at it.

We continue to do everything possible to help those most in need, and our FY16 request that you mentioned, the USAID piece of it at $735 million for the Syrian humanitarian response demonstrates that continued commitment.

Now 4 years into this conflict, Syrians see no end in sight to the violence. ISIL's abuses, including the death of Kayla Mueller you mentioned, have been layered on top of the Assad regime's indiscriminate killings and barrel bombings.

Our partners are heroically working through all possible channels, often at considerable risk, to reach those in need, including in regime areas, in opposition- and ISIL-controlled areas of Syria. For over 3 years, we have provided emergency care to nearly 2 million patients at 300 U.S.-supported health facilities throughout the area. I saw some of those patients myself last week at a hospital in Jordan.

Thanks to the aggressive vaccination campaign, by the number of polio cases in Syria is now down to zero. We have improved water and sanitation for 1.3 million Syrians, repairing water networks, installing latrines and bathrooms in camps. These efforts have helped to prevent the spread of disease.

And then, for the third year we are working tirelessly to help the most vulnerable cope with winter, especially those who are living in makeshift homes and tents. So far, we have distributed blankets, warm clothing, plastic sheeting to almost ½ million people. We have also distributed air heaters and put up windows and doors to help insulate homes.

We know that women and children are the most impacted in this crisis. And so, we also prioritize and integrate their protection into all of our humanitarian assistance efforts.

As you mentioned, the United States is the largest donor, and including the largest food donor, to the crisis, providing more than $1.1 billion worth to date to feed more than 4.8 million people inside Syria and 1.7 million in the neighboring countries. The food vouchers we provide to Syrian refugees so that they can buy locally have also injected about $1 billion into the economies of Lebanon and Jordan, Turkey, Egypt, and Iraq. In fact, within Jordan, it equals to about .7 percent of their GDP. And we have a robust system for monitoring our humanitarian assistance to ensure that it does, indeed, get to the most in-need people for whom it is intended.

We know that Syria's neighbors are stretched beyond capacity. That is why we are also helping, working in host communities, in cooperation with our State Department colleagues, to build resilient systems that can withstand the increased demand on services from the flow of refugees into their countries.

In Jordan, for instance, we are working to conserve water. With the Complex Crisis Fund resources, we have built cisterns to collect rainwater in 90 schools in Jordan and provided more than 2,200 no-interest loans, so that families can install rainwater-harvesting systems. These efforts have saved 200,000 cubic meters of water, equal to 5.5 million showers.

In Lebanon, we are working to decrease tensions between host communities and refugees. Following clashes recently between militants and Lebanese armed forces in Tripoli, our partners worked with the community to rehabilitate the old city and involved young people to reduce the appeal to extremism.

So, we are doing everything we can, but important challenges remain. Constrained access, insecurity, including targeted attacks against humanitarian workers, are a prime challenge. As Kelly mentioned, we are working with donors to try to jointly meet the overwhelming needs for resources.

Despite many challenges, we remain committed to saving lives and to helping host communities, recognizing this is a long-term crisis.

Thank you for your support. Thank you for this hearing. And again, I look forward to your questions.

[The prepared statement of Mr. Staal follows:]

**Testimony of Acting Assistant Administrator Thomas H. Staal,
U.S. Agency for International Development to the
House Foreign Affairs Subcommittee on the Middle East and North Africa and the
Subcommittee on Africa, Global Health, Global Human Rights, and International
Organizations**

"The Syrian Humanitarian Crisis Four Years Later, No End in Sight"

February 12, 2015

Introduction

Chairman Ros-Lehtinen, Ranking Member Deutch, Chairman Smith, Ranking Member Bass, and Members of the Subcommittees, thank you for the opportunity to testify today on the humanitarian crisis in Syria.

The Syrian crisis is the largest and most complex humanitarian emergency of our time. The emergence of the Islamic State of Iraq and the Levant (ISIL) has exacerbated an already protracted crisis in Syria, where the Assad regime has waged an unrelenting campaign of bloodshed against its own people for four years.

The humanitarian situation grows more complex every day. There are more than 12.2 million Syrians in need of humanitarian assistance— more than half of Syria's pre-war population, and equal to the combined populations of New York City and Los Angeles. According to the United Nations (UN), Syrians are now the largest refugee population in the world under the mandate of the UN High Commissioner for Refugees. One in five people displaced globally is Syrian.

The conflict has radically reshaped the demographics of a region with an already delicate ethnic and religious balance and scarce resources. According to UN estimates, refugees from Syria now account for one-quarter of Lebanon's population and at least 10 percent of Jordan's. Indeed, Lebanon now hosts the largest concentration of refugees in the world. This population bulge has overwhelmed basic infrastructure, including water systems, hospitals, and schools.

Last week in Jordan and Iraq, I visited Syrian partners and communities struggling to withstand another winter away from home and heard from families that had fled unspeakable horrors.

We are doing everything possible to save lives, alleviate human suffering, and restore dignity and resilience among the most vulnerable. The United States is the single largest donor of humanitarian assistance to people affected by the Syrian crisis, providing more than $3 billion to date. Our FY 2016 request of $735 million for International Disaster Assistance Overseas Contingency Operations resources for the Syrian humanitarian response demonstrates our continued commitment to the most vulnerable people and communities impacted by this tragic crisis.

Today, I'd like to cover three key areas: First, an update on the U.S. response in Syria; second, how we are building resilient systems so host communities can cope with the influx of refugees; and third, an outline of the key challenges that lie ahead.

The U.S. Response

This protracted and brutal war is testing the capacity of the humanitarian community at a time of immense global need. For the first time in USAID's history, our Office of U.S. Foreign Disaster Assistance has deployed four Disaster Assistance Response Teams (DARTs) and activated three Response Management Teams (RMTs) concurrently. Our DART for Syria is working in collaboration with partners, the UN, and other donors to coordinate our response.

Four years into the conflict, Syrians see no end in sight to the violence. ISIL's abuses, including the horrific murder of Jordanian pilot Captain Muath al-Kasasbeh last week, have been layered on top of the Assad regime's indiscriminate killings and barrel bombings, which have displaced millions. There are 9.8 million Syrians who are food insecure— lacking reliable access to affordable, nutritious food. More than half of Syria's hospitals and a quarter of its schools have been destroyed. Water availability in Syria has decreased to 50 percent of pre-crisis levels. While many internally displaced persons (IDPs) are hosted by friends or family, others are living in warehouses, poultry farms, or other structures that lack sanitation facilities and are not equipped for winter.

Our partners are heroically providing humanitarian assistance to Syrians who are most in need— including IDPs, host families, and other conflict-affected communities. Partners continue to work through all possible channels, including across international borders and conflict lines, to deliver food, medicine, relief supplies, and sanitation services in regime, opposition, and ISIL-controlled areas— wherever people are in need throughout Syria.

For over three years, the U.S. government has provided emergency care to those caught in the crossfire. Nearly two million patients have been treated for trauma wounds, received vaccines, and undergone more than 186,000 surgeries at over 300 U.S. supported hospitals, clinics, and mobile medical units across Syria this year. We have also trained 3,100 Syrian volunteers to provide emergency care. After a polio outbreak in Syria in 2013, USAID and its international partners mounted an aggressive response, supporting an unprecedented vaccination campaign across the war-torn country that helped bring polio cases down in Syria. January marked one year of no new cases.

We have improved water and sanitation for 1.3 million Syrians in all 14 governorates. Partners have organized hygiene awareness sessions and trucked water to ensure access to clean water. We are carrying out emergency repairs of water networks as well as repairs and upgrades to water sources and bathrooms in communal shelters. We are supporting solid waste collection and upgrades to temporary shelters and camps, including constructing latrines to help prevent the spread of disease. In times of crisis, clean water and sanitation are critical to survival; these programs have prevented countless illnesses and deaths.

Harsh winter weather can exacerbate already tough living conditions, but we can predict and prepare for this, given sufficient resources and access to those in need. For the third year, we are working tirelessly to support Syrians enduring another harsh winter away from home, especially those living in informal shelters. Preparations for winter began last spring. In October 2014, 18 partners began distributing supplies to prepare for the cold weather, along with other relief items. Our partners have reached almost half a million people so far this winter, through distributions that included 58,400 winter kits, 193,500 blankets and bedding kits, and 203,400 clothing kits. We have also distributed 13,900 relief vouchers so that families can buy much-needed fuel. We are providing plastic sheeting and other supplies to weather-proof makeshift homes and tents. One partner is putting up windows, doors, and glass to insulate the homes of more than 500 families in Aleppo.

We are also taking measures to prevent disease outbreaks that can arise from cold, wet weather. With our support, health facilities received 300,000 flu vaccines and antibiotics to treat common winter infections. The UN World Health Organization and other partners have provided water heaters to hospitals in eight governorates, serving more than two million people, and distributed air heaters to 800,000 people in nine governorates in Syria.

Food Assistance
The United States is the largest food donor in the Syrian crisis, providing more than $1.1 billion to date. With our help, more than 4.8 million people in Syria and 1.7 million refugees have food to eat. We take a locally appropriate and cost-effective approach to meet the diverse needs of Syrians in and out of Syria. Through the UN World Food Program (WFP) and other partners, we support family rations and flour-to-bakery programs inside Syria. In neighboring countries, WFP issues food voucher debit cards, which help restore some normalcy to refugees' lives, by allowing refugees, including many female-headed households, to buy groceries in local supermarkets. These efforts not only feed Syrian refugees, easing the pressure on host countries, but also support local economies. According to the WFP, its voucher program has injected approximately $1 billion into the economies of Lebanon, Jordan, Turkey, Egypt, and Iraq since the program began. In Jordan, the program has injected several hundred million dollars into the economy, and in Lebanon, it has created 1,300 new jobs.

WFP is taking steps to make its operations more sustainable and cost-effective through increased targeting of assistance to the most vulnerable and reducing operational costs. We applaud these efforts, and urge other donors to continue their support for the program, which provides a lifeline to so many Syrians in need, and to the economies of the region.

Women and Children
Protecting women and children is a priority for the U.S. government in all humanitarian settings, and nowhere is this more important than in the Syrian crisis. In ISIL-held areas, the group has sanctioned barbaric tactics such as stoning women and selling girls as young as 12 into sex slavery. Eighty five percent of those killed in the Syrian crisis have been men, leaving behind women heads of households struggling to keep their families alive. Nearly three million Syrian children are out of school. Behind these statistics is a generation of

girls and boys yearning to shed the trauma of conflict and build a more prosperous and peaceful future.

We have provided $26 million in humanitarian protection activities to ensure maximum safety and dignity for women. Partners distribute hygiene and infant supplies; install separate toilets and showers for women with inside locks; and build latrines near tents. We are supporting mobile clinics to increase access to reproductive health services and clinical care for survivors of Gender Based Violence (GBV) and have trained 360 healthcare workers to respond to GBV cases throughout Syria. We support safe spaces for young women to talk about the challenges they face, including early marriages, which are on the rise.

The U.S. is also expanding educational and recreational opportunities to restore a sense of normalcy for Syrian girls and boys. We provide psychosocial support and recreational opportunities for Syrian children who have suffered or are at high risk of abuse. In neighboring countries, we are ensuring that all children can keep thriving, especially in schools absorbing refugee children. In Lebanon, we are rehabilitating 259 public schools, including 131 schools in areas with a high number of Syrian refugees; providing equipment; and training teachers to improve learning outcomes. In Jordan, USAID has trained 12,700 teachers to integrate refugee children recovering from war.

Supporting Resilience in Syria's Neighbors

Many Syrian families have been uprooted more than once over the past four years. The seemingly endless flow of Syrian refugees into neighboring countries has put a massive strain on households and economies across the region. Many Jordanian and Lebanese towns along the Syrian border have doubled or tripled in size due to the influx of Syrian refugees. We commend the generosity of the Lebanese, Turkish, Jordanian, Egyptian, and Iraqi people with their Syrian neighbors. However, we are concerned with recent restrictions by Jordan and Lebanon to close or tightly manage their borders. The U.S. government continues to urge countries to keep borders open, but we understand that host communities are stretched beyond capacity and need our help. That is why we are investing more resources, in close coordination with the State Department's Bureau of Population, Refugees, and Migration, into helping these communities build resilient systems that can withstand the shocks of refugee flows. We are working with host communities across the region to improve water, healthcare, and education systems to cope with the increased demand.

Jordan is one of the most water-scarce countries in the world. Now more than ever its water system is stretched beyond capacity. Through the Complex Crises Fund, USAID is working with communities in Mafraq and Irbid— two northern towns with the heaviest concentration of refugees— to conserve water. In more than 90 schools, we have organized plays to teach children about conservation and built cisterns to collect rainwater. We have provided more than 2,200 no-interest loans to community-based cooperatives so that families can afford to install rainwater harvesting systems in their homes. These efforts saved almost 200,000 cubic meters of water— equal to 5.5 million showers. We are also helping to alleviate the strain on water and basic services in Lebanon, especially after last year's drought. As a result, over 220,000 Lebanese and Syrians had access to better waste management systems and over 265,000 had increased access to water.

We are also helping host communities to improve the delivery of basic services. In Irbid, we helped facilitate a town hall meeting where people voted on activities to improve their town, such as trash collection and road improvements. After the voting, we provided uniforms, equipment, and trash receptacles to help residents clean up the town. By involving both Jordanian and Syrian residents in these decisions, people were able to voice their frustrations and find workable solutions to make their town more livable for everyone.

We are also assisting heath facilities that are overwhelmed by the influx of patients. We are the largest donor to Jordan's health sector, where 70 percent of all deliveries now take place in public hospitals largely renovated by our partners. We have expanded access to care at more than 30 facilities.

In Lebanon, we are working to mitigate increased sectarian and host community-refugee tensions and to counter the rise of violent extremism. For example, following clashes in October between militants and Lebanese Armed Forces in Tripoli, the U.S. worked with civil society groups to rehabilitate the Old City, including a vegetable market. These efforts revived the economy in a previously marginalized and impoverished area. By talking to youth and involving them in our efforts, we sought to reduce the appeal of extremism.

Fifty-three percent of registered refugees from Syria in Lebanon are under 18, and in desperate need of educational and employment opportunities. The donor community must help Lebanon expand opportunities for its refugees, and alleviate the pressure on Lebanese host communities in order to counter the dangerous tensions that could ensnare the country in a downward spiral of insecurity and conflict.

Challenges

The U.S. government has been leading the charge to meet the overwhelming needs of those affected by the ongoing conflict in Syria, including those who have been displaced by the violence and host communities in and out of Syria. Despite our best efforts, important challenges remain, underscoring the need for increased commitments and coordination among foreign donors and humanitarian partners.

Access
Constrained access and insecurity remain the primary constraint to providing urgently needed humanitarian assistance to those in need inside Syria. The U.S. government continues to work through all possible channels— including more than 50 UN, international, and Syrian NGO partners— to meet the urgent humanitarian needs of the Syrian people. However, violence continues to hinder the delivery of assistance, including in regime-held, opposition-held, and ISIL-held areas. An estimated 4.8 million Syrians in need reside in UN-identified hard-to-reach areas, including 2.7 million residing in areas

under ISIL control. At least 150 NGO, Syrian Arab Red Crescent, and UN staff members have lost their lives providing life-saving assistance in Syria.

Host Communities
Donors must continue to work together to relieve the strain on host communities, and ensure their security. Donors, the UN, and humanitarian NGO partners must find a way forward and bolster funding commitments to support host communities across the region to build resilience, mitigate sectarian tensions, and counter violent extremism.

Conclusion

The U.S. government remains committed to keeping the lines of assistance open to save lives in Syria. And as part of our mission to ending extreme poverty and promoting resilient, democratic societies, we are committed to helping Syria's neighbors build resilient systems to cope with the strain of refugee flows, recognizing this is a long-term crisis with regional impact.

We know that humanitarian assistance cannot solve the conflict, but it is vital to keeping civilians alive. Forging strong partnerships will be crucial to the immense needs ahead. We must also find a political solution to the crisis that can ultimately stop the bloodshed, destruction, and displacement.

USAID is deeply appreciative of Congressional support that makes our work possible in Syria. Thank you for your interest, and we look forward to your questions.

Ms. ROS-LEHTINEN. Thank you. Our members thank you for your service, your dedication, your hard work in responding to this serious humanitarian crisis unfolding before us.

As you both have said, the United States plays a critical role in the international response as the largest donor country, having contributed more than $3 billion. But, as I mentioned earlier, we also have a responsibility to ensure that we are being good stewards of U.S. taxpayer money and that these funds are being used to maximize efficacy and transparency.

How much of that $3 billion has gone directly to neighboring countries or directly to NGOs and implementing partners on the ground, and how much has gone through multilateral initiatives through U.N. appeals? I will ask you to respond.

It seems that the majority of our assistance, from what I have read, actually goes to the U.N. and third-party implementing partners. Also, while it was positive that the U.N. Security Council passed Resolutions 1239 and 2165 calling upon all parties to allow delivery of humanitarian assistance and authorizing the U.N. to carry out relief delivery across these conflict lines, that is really a fanciful notion to think that the Assad regime, ISIL, al-Nusra, other belligerent actors are actually going to adhere to these resolutions. Yet, since those resolutions passed, the U.S. has been going into the war zones and the most difficult-to-reach areas of Syria.

How are these resolutions of full access being enforced? We have seen reports that ISIL and others have gotten some of this assistance or that implementing partners are forced to go through middlemen to get to some of these most dangerous areas. Do we have an idea of how much of our assistance is being co-oped by these belligerent actors or going through middlemen? What kind of visibility do we have? How can we ensure that the billions of dollars that we are providing are reaching the intended recipients and not falling into the wrong hands? And also, do we have any oversight over these U.N. agencies operate? Is there a transparency or reporting requirements for the agencies or implementing partners or is it more of a case of, well, our responsibility ends once we hand the money over to the U.N.? Finally, what are the reporting requirements for the NGOs directly funded by the U.S. Government? Do we have enough oversight mechanisms? Are they sufficient?

Thank you.

Mr. STAAL. Thank you, Chairman Ros-Lehtinen.

That is a critical question. I am really glad you brought it up because I think we actually have a good news story there.

It is always important that our aid gets to the right people. We realize the challenges in this crisis. So, we have actually upped the ante and increased our systems for overseeing that. So, in addition to the regular quarterly and annual reports, we actually require now weekly reports from our partners, where they identify particular issues.

Remember, in Syria we are working with partners that are experienced. They have worked in these kinds of areas before and know how to work in these areas. They are careful about taking risk, but they also understand the importance of oversight.

So, they have instituted multiple systems to ensure that oversight. They work through local partners, but ones that they know. They get their regular reports.

But, in addition to that, because it is a relatively-sophisticated society—Syria was a middle-income country really and people have cell phones, and so on—so, we actually have a system where, when food is delivered, they can send a picture taken from the cell phone with the barcode so we know exactly where it went and when it arrived.

Ms. ROS-LEHTINEN. Well, thank you. Let me interrupt you here a second.

Mr. STAAL. We have got multiple systems like that going on.

Ms. ROS-LEHTINEN. Let me ask about a majority of assistance. Does it go through to the U.N. and third-party implementing partners or directly to the partner?

Ms. CLEMENTS. Thank you for that question, Chairman.

About 72 percent of that $3 billion goes through U.N. mechanisms. About $750 million goes to NGOs through a joint effort really in terms of collaboration. You know our No. 1 humanitarian objective in this crisis is to get as much aid through as many channels as we possibly can. Whoever is best placed in certain circumstances are the ones that we ask to deliver, obviously, to the extent that they are comfortable delivering, given all the challenges that are actually there.

You asked, in particular, about the crossing lines and cross-border, Ranking Member Deutch. Since the resolutions have passed in the Security Council, we have had about 54 of those AID shipments reach about 600,000 people in terms of the cross-border efforts. That doesn't mean that we are keeping up with need, though. So, I don't want you to be left with a good news story. The needs are vastly outstripping the humanitarian aid that we are able to provide.

Tom mentioned the enhanced monitoring. We, too, on the U.N., at least the U.N. Refugee Agency and others that we support, have asked for enhanced monitoring plans.

Ms. ROS-LEHTINEN. Thank you.

Ms. CLEMENTS. In terms of diversion——

Ms. ROS-LEHTINEN. My time is up.

Ms. CLEMENTS. Okay.

Ms. ROS-LEHTINEN. And we have votes on the floor.

But would you like for me to recognize you or we will break? Mr. Deutch?

Mr. DEUTCH. Just for one observation. We have to go the floor for votes.

But before we leave, I just wanted to say that listening to the two of you give your testimony and respond to the chair's questions I think reminds us that, it is a good reminder of why we are proud to be Americans.

Ms. ROS-LEHTINEN. Amen.

Thank you very much. Excellent work.

And we will be back, and Mr. Smith will chair the remainder of the hearing.

With that, our subcommittees are in recess. Thank you.

[Recess.]

Mr. SMITH [presiding]. The hearing will resume its sitting, and we will be joined by Mr. Deutch, who is under a time constraint. I will yield to him when he comes back for any questions he might have.

But let me, first of all, thank you again for the tremendous work you are doing in saving lives. I think sometimes people are very critical of foreign aid. They should know the robust efforts you, the administration, the Congress in a supportive role, are undertaking to save lives of the most precious and the most vulnerable people, particularly women and children. So, again, let me echo what we all said, I think, in our openings, just how grateful we all are for the work that you are doing for people who have been displaced, the refugees, the IDPs, women and children who are being savagely attacked and women who have been raped.

I will never forget years ago during the Balkan wars I had hearings with women who had been raped. One, she was so traumatized and she thought she could handle speaking what other women were experiencing during the Balkan wars. Bianca Jagger was actually here as well speaking to that. And she froze; she couldn't speak. She had been so utterly traumatized.

And I know you are helping women who have been so horrifically violated. So, thank you for that as well.

I do have a question. Secretary Clements, Deputy Assistant Secretary, you mentioned with regards to the vaccination 2.9 million children require lifesaving vaccinations. I wonder if you could break that out a little bit. They have not gotten it or some of those have already received it? What vaccinations are we talking about?

I have always believed that vaccinations like antibiotics as well as anesthesia are among the wonders of the world in terms of how they mitigate disease and pain. So, the question would be, 2.9 million, what are they lacking and what is being done to try to get those vaccinations to them?

Ms. CLEMENTS. Thank you very much, Chairman Smith, and thanks for your kind words.

I have to say, to follow up on a point that the ranking member made before he left, it is a moment to be proud as an American in terms of what the U.S. taxpayer is doing to help us provide this kind of humanitarian aid to so many people in need. We deeply appreciate that.

In terms of the vaccination question—and we can take that and get some more granularity for you certainly——

Mr. SMITH. Great.

Ms. CLEMENTS [continuing]. But between USAID and the State Department's humanitarian programs, both inside Syria as well as in the neighboring countries, a very strong network of health providers. And obviously, through UNICEF and through the World Health Organization, with a large number of implementers, there has been a great effort underway to try to vaccinate as many kids as possible. I can speak more to the refugee side of things in terms of in the neighboring countries, but it is a core part of the health services that we are providing every day.

Mr. STAAL. Yes, thanks for that question. It is important.

I mentioned the polio vaccination, and that an indication that they are actually able to get out to a lot of places that you might not think they could. It is still not perfect, and we continue to try to get as far as we can.

Last week when I was in Jordan, I visited one of our implementing partners. They have been able to establish and are continuing to expand their network of field hospitals and clinics in opposition-held areas from across the border. That is another way we can start to push out the reach of healthcare, including vaccination. But that is a critical issue, yes.

Mr. SMITH. Let me ask you a question. I mean, we all know from history that the Spanish flu epidemic, of course, had nothing to do with Spain, but it was a terrible pandemic. Following World War I, it infected some 500 million people. The estimates are upwards of 50 million, some say more, some say less, actually died, 5 percent of the world's population.

Health services have been disrupted with more than 73 percent of hospitals, 27 percent of primary healthcare facilities, and 65 to 70 percent of the pharmaceutical companies out of service. A couple of weeks ago, I met with Dr. Peter Hotez, who has been here before to testify. He is the leader on neglected tropical diseases. As a matter of fact, I have a pending bill that we wrote with his very, very insightful suggestions on what it should look like.

But I know he has said that he has concerns that a pandemic could arise out of Syria or the region, war conditions, lack of sanitation, cholera, all the other attendant problems. The longer this conflict goes on—and again, the Spanish flu occurred near the end or at the end of all of the blood-letting in World War I. I am just wondering what your thoughts might be on that. I know we are far more advanced than they were back in 1918. But when we and people like you don't have access to contested areas or healthcare workers are being killed simply because they are trying to assist, it makes it harder and these things could happen. What are your thoughts on that?

Ms. CLEMENTS. I wonder sometimes whether or not you have read so much into my bio that you know that my husband works on pandemic preparedness at USAID, actually.

In terms of this, obviously, it is a huge concern. You know, with the war that has raged on now for over 4 years, the concern in terms of the health system inside Syria, losing 30 years in that time at least. As you well know, the medical facilities and the personnel delivering those services have been under attack. Until very recently, actually, even in some of the cross-border/cross-line operations, some of the partners we are trying to get aid out to could not put any kind of medical health into their kits, into the aid that they were delivering in communities. So, it is a real concern.

I think we do the best we can in terms of the areas we can access. I think our support systems are much stronger in the neighboring countries; in Jordan, in particular, in Lebanon, and the Iraqi Kurdistan region, and so on, in terms of what we are trying to do. Obviously, Turkey has done a tremendous amount on the health side. But that is something that we need to continue to work on, to try to prevent what you have just outlined.

Mr. STAAL. And I might add, it is all the more reason why it is important that this U.N. resolution last year, 2165, being able to work across borders, so organizations like WHO, then, can move across those lines of conflict. We need to continue to support that.

The other maybe helpful mitigating factor is that Syrians are used to getting vaccination and they demand it. Okay? Some refugees we work with or people in underdeveloped countries are not used to it. They are used to it. And so, they are looking for vaccination, and that does help mitigate some of the problems.

Mr. SMITH. Ranking Member Deutch?

Mr. DEUTCH. Thank you, Mr. Chairman.

Thanks again to both of you and thanks for being so patient and for allowing us to do the other part of our job.

Ms. Clements, I would like to ask you about another issue that I have raised several times in this committee. What are we doing to increase our support from the international community? It is really frustrating, as I said in my opening statement and as you referred to as well, it is frustrating to learn that last year's U.N. appeal was only 50 percent funded. It is clear that, even if there is a political agreement, if there were a political agreement tomorrow in Syria, the humanitarian crisis is going for years to come. So, how do we get our partners around the world to not only to continue to care about the humanitarian crisis and talk about the humanitarian crisis, but to actually do their part to help alleviate the suffering?

Ms. CLEMENTS. Thank you very much, Congressman.

This is the key issue. We have in terms of the Syria crisis right now appeal levels of $8.4 billion. I mean, that is more than $2 billion more than last year. We are approaching a year where we are dealing with—and we have talked about this a little bit—the global humanitarian crises. We have Sudan. We have C.A.R. We have Iraq. I mean, all of that adds to the attention that is being diverted somewhat from this crisis. So, I think it is very important, for example, for this hearing to take place and to continue to bring attention to it.

We have worked very hard with other governments, with traditional and non-traditional donors, to try to increase support. Obviously, we continue that effort. Tom and I were actually in Kuwait City about 10 days ago at a top donors' group meeting that was hosted by Kuwait to try to bring attention to the Syrian response, what we are going to do this year, and perhaps even more importantly, what comes next year and the year after. Given that this is going to be protracted, we need to continue that support, for example, to Jordan and to the other neighbors that are shouldering the burden.

So, it is a very high priority. There is a lot of engagement at very senior levels of our Government, and that will continue.

Mr. DEUTCH. And what is that? What is the response? I appreciate that there is engagement.

Ms. CLEMENTS. I think, as I outlined in terms of the number of crises, the places that we are asking people to put their money, unfortunately, it is increasing rather than decreasing. We have seen, for example, Saudi Arabia, when WFP, as you mentioned in your opening statement, had their fundraising campaign in December, it was Saudi Arabia that stepped forward with I think $72 million to help to close that gap. That was unexpected.

We just saw the EU last week announce a $1 billion package for both development and humanitarian support. The UK, the visit of Prince Charles and the Secretary of State, just announced another 100 million pounds.

So, we are seeing donors step forward. The problem is we are not able to get to the levels, the astronomical levels, now in terms of trying to meet the need.

Mr. DEUTCH. Okay. I would just make the observation that we are about to begin a debate about AUMF to combat ISIS. We are devoting an enormous amount of resources on security in the region already, in addition to the security arrangements that we have within the region that benefit, in particular, those countries that we have asked to step up in providing humanitarian assistance. I trust that in terms of engagement that those points are made loudly and clearly to our allies when we have those discussions.

Mr. Staal, I want to return to a topic that I focused on in each of the hearings that we have had on humanitarian needs. I would just love an update. That is the issue of branding.

Chairman Ros-Lehtinen and I visited the Zaatari Camp in Jordan this past summer, and we saw temporary housing stamped with a green flag, the Saudi Arabian flag, many other donor countries. We didn't see a lot of U.S. flags. And I understand the difficulties of branding inside Syria, and we would never want to put AID workers at risk. But in refugee camps and in communities, have we increased U.S. branding, so that the Syrian people know that they have the full support of the United States?

Mr. STAAL. Yes, thank you very much for that question, Ranking Member Deutch.

It is an issue that we continue to discuss with our partners. As you mentioned, inside Syria it is very dangerous. And so, we don't require that.

Within the surrounding countries, we are asking them to step up their branding. It may not be on every bag because some of that goes into Syria and some doesn't. So, it is difficult to differentiate. But at least to put up more signs around and portray that.

Also, just in discussions with the officials who are working in those camps to make sure they understand where the assistance is coming from, and, in fact, we are able to do that even inside Syria, in a quiet way to let people know the local organizations that we are working with, where it comes from, to get the word out.

Mr. DEUTCH. All right. Great.

Ms. Clements?

Ms. CLEMENTS. A quick add, because we are very familiar with the Zaatari example. We have had a number of discussions, actually, with UNHCR, Andrew Harper, in particular, about the visibility issues related to Zaatari.

The challenge has been, as soon as a U.S. flag goes up, it comes down. And so, we have a requirement, actually, in our contributions that U.S. flags should be on items that we have actually supported, particularly, for example, in Jordan and northern Iraq, places where it is quite safe and we want to get the word out. But it is a challenge keeping it visible for extended periods of time.

Mr. DEUTCH. Okay. I appreciate it.

Thank you to the witnesses. Again, I would just ask if you would please pass on our sincere thanks and appreciation to all of those on whose behalf you appear here today. Thank you.

Mr. SMITH. Thank you very much.

Mr. Meadows?

Mr. MEADOWS. Yes, thank you, Mr. Chairman.

And thank each of you for being here. This particular issue is not as telling from a standpoint of getting the American people to act as perhaps other things that we see on TV on a regular basis. But, yet, when it comes to asking for people to give, either personally or allow their government to give on their behalf, it is the one thing that typically can unite people on both sides of the aisle.

The American people are very generous and caring and giving people. It is hard for them, Ms. Clements, when you make statements like, well, the American flag goes up and it gets ripped down. It also makes it very difficult for a lot of people to continue to say, why give money for humanitarian purposes when they don't care?

So, getting back to the branding issue that the ranking member was talking about, I think it is important for us to tell the stories of the impact on the lives that we really are affecting. Because not only in Syria and Jordan and some of the other places where the refugee and the migration from this conflict is huge, we are making real-life differences to moms and dads and kids. We have got to do a better job of sharing that, if we can.

And so, I guess my question to both of you is, how, as a Member of Congress, can we do that? As either NGOs or the like, how can we do a better job of thanking the American taxpayer back home and telling the stories? I mean, we see ads all the time of starving children, and people willing give because they believe that they are making a difference. How can we do a better job of that?

Ms. CLEMENTS. Thank you very much, Congressman.

I actually could not have said it better than the way you just did in terms of telling individual stories. Because I think with the way that this war has raged on and the number of people it has affected, that, unfortunately, the public has become numb to the numbers. And so, to try to pull out those stories of people who are actually assisting and what important work the partners that we are supporting are providing every day under difficult circumstances, to try to disentangle saving lives from the broader morass of extremist takeover of certain communities and Assad's aggressions, and that sort of think, if we can keep it focused very much on the lifesaving, we might have a better chance.

Unfortunately, we have those pictures to go along——

Mr. MEADOWS. Sure.

Ms. CLEMENTS [continuing]. With the devastation. But the individual stories I think tell the best story.

Mr. MEADOWS. Okay.

Mr. STAAL. If I might add, Congressman Meadows, thank you very much for that question. It is sometimes tough. I know I have got relatives back home and they ask, okay, what is happening with all this assistance? You know, there is a big story and, then, there are the individuals. As you say, that is so important.

In the big story, even though you have got 12 million people displace, yet there has been really no major malnutrition problems. We had a small outbreak of polio, but that was quickly stopped. And so, from a lifesaving thing, nobody froze to death because of the winter. We were able to get winterization. So, on a big scale, actually, it is pretty good.

Then, even in our protection programs, for instance, we have been training women in peacekeeping. It has actually made a difference. Okay? There is a place like in what they call Rif Dimashq—it is sort of the rural areas around Damascus—with women peace circles, they were able to negotiate 20-day ceasefires.

In the eastern Kurdish region, the women negotiated an end to price-fixing that some of the merchants were doing. So, they were able to step in and make a real difference to people on the ground that way.

Then, when I visited the hospital in northern Jordan where they are getting refugees coming out who have been injured, it is not only medical support, but we are actually providing psychosocial support. I visited with a small child that had been injured. Obviously, they had not only the physical injuries, but the psychological injuries. Part of our work was supporting and training women who, then, provide psychosocial support to that child, so that their issues can be dealt with.

Mr. MEADOWS. Well, let me close with a sincere thank you for your work, but also a request. On those individual stories like the story you just shared, if you can get that to committee, most of the Members of Congress can tweet out, Facebook out, and reach hundreds of thousands of people.

Mr. STAAL. Sure.

Mr. MEADOWS. And if we can help tell that story, because if we don't, the American people will grow weary of giving. If they don't see that they are making a difference, it will become very difficult to continue to fund worthwhile projects.

So, thank you both.

And I yield back. I thank you for your leadership, Mr. Chairman.

Mr. SMITH. Thank you very much, Mr. Meadows.

Mr. Higgins? Oh, he left. I am sorry.

Ms. Frankel?

Ms. FRANKEL. Thank you, Mr. Chair.

I thank you for your service and for your testimony today.

I know that humanitarian aid, by its nature, the purpose is to save lives and alleviate suffering, maintain human dignity. I was interested in your discussion with Mr. Deutch because I have heard people say that, if you give them food and medicine, that helps shape people's minds also.

So, my question is the overriding goal of trying to defeat ISIS and Assad, and so forth, I want to understand how the humanitarian aid plays into that. Do the folks who are receiving the aid, do they know that it is coming from—do they have any idea where it is coming from? And this humanitarian aid helps shape their thoughts or ideas, in your opinion?

Mr. STAAL. Yes, thank you. That is an important question, not always easy to quantify. Certainly, through our aid programs, even within Syria, our partners are working through local organizations.

They make sure that the local organizations know, even though it is not branded, that they know that it is coming from the U.S. and that it is U.S. taxpayers that are providing the funding for that. So, the word is getting out, not as much as we would like, and it is an ongoing challenge, but I think that it is important.

I think part of it is, yes, you have to provide the immediate humanitarian assistance, but you also need to do it as much as possible in a way that protects their dignity. Okay? And so, we are trying as much as possible to move to a system of distribution of our assistance that just doesn't make them totally dependent on hand-outs.

So, that is part of the reason we have gone to these ration cards. I actually have one in my pocket here. That way, instead of getting a bag of rice and a can of vegetable oil, they get a card. They can go to a supermarket and buy the goods that they think they need. That gives them a little feeling of dignity, and, of course, it helps thelocaleconomy.

Ms. FRANKEL. May I just change—oh, wait, you can answer that. Why don't you answer the other question that I have also, which is this: In terms of our AID workers, first of all, do we have AID workers in Syria? Given what we just saw happen with Kayla Mueller, I think we all have a concern whether our AID workers in the region are safe. Could you also speak to that?

Ms. CLEMENTS. Maybe if I could just respond to the last and let Tom——

Ms. FRANKEL. Yes, please do that.

Ms. CLEMENTS [continuing]. Respond on the other?

I think it was Congressman Boyle that mentioned this being a regional issue. Often, when Tom and I are talking about Syria, we will talk about Iraq, too, because we do actually view this as very much a regional issue.

We, in terms of the anti-ISIL fight, humanitarian support is one of those lines of efforts, but it is not to battle ISIL. It is to aid those victims and those people in need. So, we try very much to keep it as a needs focus as opposed to part of the fight. So, it is a distinction that is very important to protect the safety of humanitarian workers, allow us to continue to save lives. I just wanted to make thatclear.

Ms. FRANKEL. Good. Okay. Thank you for that.

Can you answer the question on the safety?

Mr. STAAL. Yes, thank you, Congresswoman Frankel.

Certainly, it is a dangerous place. I think I mentioned in my written testimony 150 humanitarian workers have been killed over the last 3 years. It is something that we continually have on our minds.

The partners that we are working with and through, both U.N. and international NGOs, are all ones that are well-experienced in working these kinds of regions and these conflict areas. So, they are even more careful than we are.

They work primarily through local partners, the NGOs. Some of the U.N. folks are there in Damascus, especially in the government-held areas. But in the opposition areas it is primarily the NGOs. They, in turn, work through local organizations. So, there are very few of our international staff going in. It is more focused with the local organizations who know the scene.

Ms. FRANKEL. And this is in Syria?

Mr. STAAL. In Syria, yes.

Ms. FRANKEL. Thank you, Mr. Chair.

Mr. SMITH. Thank you, Ms. Frankel.

The Chair recognizes Mr. Yoho.

Mr. YOHO. Thank you, Mr. Chairman.

I appreciate your testimony today.

You were stating that America is largest single donor in that region, and then, Mr. Staal, you were saying that you have, in virtually all the places you have looked, you have not found people starving. Did I understand that correctly. But are you talking about the refugees that are outside of Syria or the ones within Syria that you work with? Because reading my notes here, it says there are a lot of nutritionally-deprived people there. What is the dichotomy of the difference there visibly? I mean, is it distinctive?

Mr. STAAL. Yes, thank you very much, Congressman Yoho.

It is an important distinction. Certainly, within Syria they are worse off than outside of Syria, and they are nutritionally-deprived, but they aren't to the point of starvation.

Mr. YOHO. Okay, and that leads into my other question.

Mr. STAAL. Yes.

Mr. YOHO. When you are going in and trying to get access into Syria, are you running—I mean, you have got to worry about the Assad government forces and, then, you have got to worry about Freedom Fighters and ISIS and all those other ones.

It just seems like one of the things I have seen on these other meetings that we have had, in particular, I think it was Afghan last year when we were talking to Dr. Shah. He said that Afghan was allocated or appropriated $1 billion in foreign aid through USAID, but they couldn't account for $300 million.

As you are going from taking our aid—and I would feel a lot better if it was branded. That is the American taxpayers' money, and I agree with these other people that, if we are sending our money over there, well, I think they need to know where it is coming from. I know that is an issue in itself because it causes resentment. But, as you go into those areas, what are the biggest obstacles you are running into to make sure that we have accountability of those products, or whatever it is you are taking in there, and that it is not falling into hands where they are using it to raise revenues?

Mr. STAAL. Yes, thank you. That is an important issue that we track very carefully.

The branding issue, it is less about the resentment; it is more about the protection of our partners. Because if they are seen as working for the Americans, then that could put them in danger. So, that is the real issue, rather than the resentment issue.

Mr. YOHO. How do other countries handle that? This is another question. We have given $3 billion since the beginning of this. The collection of other countries, have they come close to that as far as monetary input? Ms. Clements?

Ms. CLEMENTS. Sure. Actually, we are about 30 percent of the overall giving last year, was from the United States.

Mr. YOHO. Okay.

Ms. CLEMENTS. And collectively, we are, obviously, the largest single donor. But, no, it is burden-sharing.

Mr. YOHO. Okay. So, you are seeing other countries step up and help out?

Ms. CLEMENTS. Yes.

Mr. YOHO. This is only going to get worse until we have a resolution to the problem within Syria. I think it is going to wind up being a regime change, which at this point I think the rest of the world would be safer off and the people of Syria, obviously.

When you are going in and you are putting in, say, water, are you building infrastructures or are you just taking supplies in, like bottled water? I saw you had Jerrycans and all that stuff. Are you putting in wells, septic tanks, or sewer systems?

Mr. STAAL. Yes, that is a critical question. Thank you very much.

We are, indeed, putting in some small-scale infrastructure as much as possible, where we can, in opposition-held areas and even in some of the government areas. But it is at a small scale, but, certainly, we are doing it, both water and other types of local infrastructure, repairing health clinics, schools, things like that.

Mr. YOHO. Okay, and when you go in there, like in a host country that is housing the refugees, is the government working with you or are you finding them an impediment of making the situation better?

Mr. STAAL. No, I was just referring now to within Syria.

Mr. YOHO. Okay.

Mr. STAAL. But, certainly, in the surrounding countries, in Jordan, in Lebanon, and other, the neighboring countries, we have really stepped up our programs. In Jordan, for instance, we have even put in a second Deputy Director for USAID and increased our assistance to the Jordanians to build up their systems to handle this big, huge influx.

Mr. YOHO. Okay.

Mr. STAAL. So, you know, additional schools, additional water systems, and so on.

Mr. YOHO. Well, I appreciate the work you are doing—and I will get right back to you—that you are doing. If you could over the course of the work you do over the next, let's say, 2 or 3 months, let us know what we can do better here to help you do better there, especially on the accountability, so that we are not wasting our money.

Ms. Clements, you had something to say?

Ms. CLEMENTS. Thank you. We really do appreciate the support. It is hugely needed.

Just on the water issue, both inside Syria—Tom had mentioned part of it, but I will give you an example. The International Committee of the Red Cross, for example, has worked very closely to try to put stop-gap measures in place to actually make clean water available for about 10 million people. This is not building big waste treatment plants, that sort of thing. It is just trying to get the system that currently exists to function. So, that is just an example of support that has been tremendously important, yes.

Mr. SMITH. Mr. Yoho, thank you.

In follow up to your question, could you provide the committee a breakdown of what each country has pledged and how much they have actually lived up to their commitment? And secondly, for this new round, what countries are pledging, so we can get it? I mean, 30 percent is certainly very, very generous on the part of the American public, the administration, and Congress, but it would be nice to know where the laggards are and where those—as you mentioned, Saudi Arabia stepped up on the food issue. So that we have contacts, all of us, all the time with people from these countries. It would be good to say, "Hey, do more" or "Well done." So, if you could provide that, that would be very helpful.

Mr. STAAL. If I can just respond to that, Chairman Smith, at the end of March, the Kuwaitis have already invited the donors to come to Kuwait for a major pledging conference for Syria and the neighboring countries. We are already encouraging our friends out there to be ready to step up with some major contributions.

Mr. SMITH. Would a letter from Members of Congress, a bipartisan letter, be of any help in terms of backing what you are trying to accomplish?

Mr. STAAL. Yes.

Mr. SMITH. If you could give us some insights on how you think that might boost the aggregate——

Mr. STAAL. Right.

Mr. SMITH [continuing]. It would be——

Mr. STAAL. Especially to the parliaments of some of the countries that we work with, yes.

Mr. SMITH. Okay. Very good point.

Ms. Frankel?

Ms. FRANKEL. Thank you again.

I have a different point of view here. So, yes, thank you again for your testimony.

I wanted to just follow up on a line of questioning that I had when I was sitting at the other end of the table. This is one way to move up in rankings, right? Send everybody else away.

I think I understand your testimony of separating the humanitarian effort from the fight against certain forces. So, my question is in Syria, for example, ISIL or Assad, are their forces, do they try to keep the humanitarian aid from getting to the Syrians? That is one question.

Mr. STAAL. Yes, that is a very important question, and it is something we watch carefully and our partners, again.

As I mentioned earlier, we actually have some pretty robust systems that are really tracking our aid very carefully, literally truckload-by-truckload that goes in there. And so, we have a very good idea of where it is going.

There has been very little pressure really to divert or try to control it. When it does happen, the partners we are working with, they are experienced. They have worked in Afghanistan, in Iraq, in South Sudan, in Somalia, and places like this. So, they push back very hard.

If it gets to the point where they feel they have to pay a bribe or allow some of it to go to a local official, they will just stop, and we don't go into that town. That has happened. There are times when we just say, okay, we can't work there. But, then, the surrounding towns continue to get it, and then, we find they come back and say, okay, well, we will let it in after all.

Ms. FRANKEL. Did you want to respond to that? Yes.

Ms. CLEMENTS. I would. I would. Thank you very much.

Yes, they are inhibiting humanitarian aid workers from delivering aid. Just to give you an example, we talked earlier in the hearing about those in besieged areas, about 212,000 that are in besieged. About 145,000 of them are besieged by the regime. So, they are not allowing aid workers or aid organizations to get in.

We probably come closest to your example of starvation in a place like Yarmouk, the Palestinian refugee camp, where it has been extremely difficult, for example, for the Palestinian U.N. Agency to get in and actually provide health and food, and so on.

So, it is administrative obstacles, bureaucratic obstacles, you know, bombs, barrel bombing in terms of just not being able to get into key areas. But it has been a huge issue.

Thank you.

Ms. FRANKEL. And in the surrounding regions, which countries are actually helping you or assisting, both with resources, but actually are friendly toward the efforts?

Ms. CLEMENTS. We are so fortunate to have the neighbors that we do surrounding Syria. I mean, we could go through them one-by-one, but Jordan, first and foremost, 650,000 registered refugees, probably many more that are in communities. Most are being supported outside of those two camps that are in Jordan. Billions of dollars spent in terms of GDP or lost economic revenue, and so on.

There has been a tremendous outpouring of generosity and support from these neighbors to welcome refugees in, but the welcome mat is starting to wear thin because of how many refugees there are and the needs and the burdens, and so on, in terms of the economic system and the infrastructure and water and health, education, you name it. But I think in every circumstance of those five we have support from the government in terms of being able to help us help them in terms of responding to these massive needs.

Ms. FRANKEL. So, I think what I hear you saying, also, is that—and you may have said this before—is that this humanitarian aid not only is to reduce suffering and dignity, and so forth, but giving relief to some of these neighboring countries that will prevent their destabilization. Okay.

Ms. CLEMENTS. It is a really important point, Congresswoman, because we try very hard not just to target aid toward the refugees or the displaced, but also the host communities. And aid in state programs in the partners we are serving, it is very much a dual approach because we do not want to increase tensions, and we see tensions rising. As you said, it is absolutely essential for regional stability.

Ms. FRANKEL. Thank you very much, Mr. Chair. I yield the rest of my time.

Mr. SMITH. Just a few final questions, and then, if my colleagues have any further, if you would answer those?

As I think you may know, I am the prime author of the Trafficking Victims Protection Act of 2000. It is a very aggressive law that seeks to prevent/prosecute traffickers and protect women and children especially who are overwhelmingly the victims.

Syria is a Tier 3 country. In the recommendations page of the TIP Report, it talks about child soldiers. I am wondering if you could shed any light on how many child soldiers we are talking about from either side or any side.

In your testimony, Mr. Staal, you very strongly pointed to the barbarity of selling girls as young as 12 into sex slavery. I am wondering if any of those girls are being rescued. How many are we talking about, just like how many child soldiers are we talking about? Is there any guesstimate as to how much of this abuse is going on?

And what happens when there is a rescue? You know, some young 12-year-old who has been so brutally abused finds their way particularly in the area of psychological treatment. You mentioned that generally before, those who are suffering trauma of war.

And I am wondering, too, an additional question: Is our response integrating a faith-based response, Muslim or Christian, with best practices for psychological help? You know, one of the things I have learned being in trafficking shelters all over the world is that the healing process, the sense of personal reconciliation with the trauma and coming to a point where you reconcile with that you are a victim, you are not in any way responsible for this, happens more effectively in a faith-based setting where there is also the best psychological practices by psychologists or psychiatrists being employed. I am wondering what we are doing along those lines. And again, if you could, speak to the trafficking part. Mr. Staal?

Mr. STAAL. Yes, thank you. Critical issues that you raise, Chairman Smith.

As I mentioned, in all of our humanitarian assistance programs we include protection issues. In addition to that, we have put in $26 million specifically in protection programs, gender-based violence issues, child protection, and so on.

Included as a piece of that has been tracking abuses that could someday be a way of keeping records that could someday be used later, as you mentioned, with the ICC, or whatever. And then, also, the State Department DRL program is continuing to try to track those kinds of abuses for future issues.

We will have to get back to you on the child soldiers. I don't know that we have a number on that.

Mr. SMITH. Are you coordinating with the TIP office on this with regards to Syria?

Mr. STAAL. Yes.

Ms. CLEMENTS. Yes. Perhaps I can respond in terms of the trafficking piece because, obviously, this is something that is of high priority to us, as it obviously is to you as well.

All of our programs actually have a GBV or prevention element. When I say that, you know, protection is important. There are a couple of things that we have tried to do very explicitly.

Civil registration and identity documents, because often we find that those instances of trafficking are because they don't have something to be able to provide for themselves in terms of livelihoods, or what have you. So, we have made a special effort through partners to be sure that that is certainly in place.

We have found that the best defense is robust assistance. So, making sure kids are in school, for example, that information is flowing in terms of the dangers of early marriage, these sorts of things all combined have a comprehensive approach to try to at least decrease the scourge.

But, yes, in fact, I was just talking with the trafficking office yesterday about this very issue.

Mr. SMITH. That would be great. Any further for the record that you could provide on that, simply as it relates to sex trafficking and child soldiers, that would be greatly appreciated.

You have pointed out that 85 percent of those killed are men. I am wondering with regard to the women, and especially pregnant women, are they getting to safe venues to have their children? Do they have access to safe blood, for example, if there is an obstructed delivery, to a Caesarean section, or has maternal mortality gone up because of the lack of that in Syria, the way that we have seen in other war-torn areas?

Mr. STAAL. Yes, a critical question. I think we have a partial answer, but not a great answer. I mean, I think there are still a lot of women who aren't able to get to a proper facility. As you have mentioned, health facilities have been targeted, especially by the regime. That has really reduced our ability to help.

On the other hand, that is a major focus of some of our programs. I mentioned earlier that the hospital I visited in Jordan last week, they have an outreach program and are setting up field hospitals in opposition-held areas in southern Syria. And so, those kinds of things we are trying to address that issue.

But, you know, certainly, in ISIL-held areas, we are not able to get there and provide that kind of assistance. It is an ongoing problem; no question.

Mr. SMITH. Just a few final questions, if I could. You mentioned, Mr. Staal, that history has been made in the number of DARTS. As you have said, four Disaster Assistance Response Teams and three Response Management Teams have been deployed. Could you elaborate on that? Because many people, particularly those watching, the C–SPAN audience, for example, you know, what is a DART?

I have actually been in areas where they have been in operation, and it is amazing how effectively they coordinate. If you could elaborate on that?

Mr. STAAL. Yes, thank you, Chairman Smith. That is one of the things that I think we, as Americans, can be most proud of. That is a unique aspect of our humanitarian assistance that other countries can't do.

That is to actually put people on the ground within hours and days of a crisis, whether it is a tsunami and an earthquake, or in this situation a conflict-related crisis. So, DART is a Disaster Assistance Response Team, and we send them out to the affected area literally within hours or days, sometimes even, if we know there is a big typhoon coming, we will send them out a day or two ahead of time.

And they include whatever is needed in terms of technical specialties. They coordinate the assistance. Ebola, for instance, we have a huge DART there. We coordinate the assistance provided by CDC, the World Health Organization, other donors. The DART provides that platform, and it works great.

The RMT, the Response Management Team, is the operation center back here at headquarters that provides all the support that responds to your questions about what is going on and to our leaders in the administration. So, it provides that sort of op center for that.

And so, we have a DART for Iraq, a DART for Syria that has people both in Jordan and in Turkey. We have a DART for South Sudan, and then, we have the huge DART for Ebola.

Mr. SMITH. Thank you for that explanation and for that work.

You point out in your testimony, Mr. Staal, that we have improved water and sanitation for 1.3 million Syrians in all 14 governorates. You are absolutely right; in times of crisis, clean water and sanitation are critical to survival.

How integrated or how expansive is our ORT, the Oral Rehydration Therapy, salts, those packets being disseminated for children especially, since diarrheal disease is one of the leading killers of children?

Mr. STAAL. Yes, thank you.

I don't have the exact details. If you like, I can try to track those down.

Mr. SMITH. We would like that, yes.

Mr. STAAL. But it is certainly a part of whatever we do in our health, in our WASH programs where we are working. There are still areas we can't reach. But, as I said, I think it is important that our humanitarian assistance also address some of those sort of resilience issues, so that people are not as dependent on humanitarian assistance.

If they have got clean water, then they are less likely to get sick. If we have got a program providing flour to bakeries across-line, so that people can get bread, that also helps the economy. So, we try to do our humanitarian assistance in a way that builds resilience, reduces cost, and then, reaches out to the people.

Mr. SMITH. You have testified that 9.8 million Syrians are food-insecure. Is that number declining or worsening?

Mr. STAAL. Yes, I think I will have to look at the exact details, but I am afraid to say it is probably worsening. Their situation is declining because of the scale of the crisis.

Mr. SMITH. And one final question. You have pointed out that, since 2011, PRM has expended $1.4 billion. Has that impacted funding from other programs? Have you had to deplete some accounts or draw down from other accounts? And have those accounts been replenished, whether it be in Africa or anywhere else, so that there is no diminution of assistance to those other crisis areas?

Ms. CLEMENTS. Thank you very much, Chairman, for the question.

It is thanks to you and Congress that I can that we have not taken funding from Africa or other important programs to meet some of those other mega humanitarian emergencies, because you appropriated a generous amount to us in 2013, 2014, and again in 2015. So, we appreciate that hugely. And you will see in terms of numbers on our congressional presentation document a significant upturn, not just in the Middle East, but in other regions as well.

Mr. SMITH. Thank you.

Ms. Frankel?

Ms. FRANKEL. Thank you, Mr. Chair.

I want to go back to my questioning on sort of, I guess, the domino effects of humanitarian aid or not having it. I do believe in humanitarian aid, but I want to sort of just play the devil's advocate because of what we may hear constituents saying. I think some of my colleagues mentioned it.

There is so much suffering in this world all over the world, including the United States of America. And so, I would like to hear your thoughts again in terms of, what if we did not provide this aid? What are some of the dominos? What would we see happening? What would be worse? What is the spinoff, and how does it affect, you know, somebody who lives in Florida?

Ms. CLEMENTS. It is a terrific question, Congresswoman.

In terms of not being able to provide aid, we touched on it a little bit earlier in terms of regional stability. I think in terms of humanitarian aid the best way to be able to support those that need to flee Syria is being able to provide that aid to the host communities and the neighboring countries to keep that protection space open, to make it possible for people, because it is much easier for us to assist those in Jordan and in Lebanon, frankly, than it is inside Syria.

You would see an implosion. You would see massive malnutrition rates, for example, in terms of global acute malnutrition, mortality rates through the roof. Most of the deaths now, unfortunately, are because of the war. We would probably see in terms of social indicators a much larger humanitarian catastrophe without aid.

Mr. STAAL. Yes, and I might add, obviously, if possible, we want to try to get our assistance to people in their homes, so they don't have to flee. They need to be able to flee if they feel they have to, but it is better to get it there. And then, that reduces the strain on the surrounding countries.

As you mentioned, Jordan is a critical partner for us. The same with Lebanon; we are very concerned about their stability—in those countries that is critical—and frankly, terrorism.

You know, a young man growing up, he can't feed his family. He hasn't got a job. He is going to be much more open to the lure, if you will, of people asking him to do bad things.

Ms. FRANKEL. Thank you very much. I think I got my question answered.

Mr. SMITH. Thank you, Ms. Frankel.

Mr. Yoho?

Mr. YOHO. Yes, going back to the aid that you are giving, when you go into the different countries, there is Turkey, Syria, Lebanon, Jordan, Iraq where the refugees are going. When you are going into the different countries, like say Turkey, you know, the human rights that we stand by, that we believe in this country, are going to be different in those other countries. Is that correct? You know, freedom of religion, freedom of expression, those kinds of things.

And so, when Chairman Smith brought up the different areas of abuses, like gender abuse, women's rights, and things like that, how do you go about enforcing that? And is it different between country to country? How do we hold that government accountable?

Mr. STAAL. That is an interesting and important question, Congressman.

I can't remember whether it was you or Chairman Smith who asked about working with faith-based organizations. We do work with that. In fact, Ms. Clements and I visited with the Archbishop in Kurdistan when we were there to talk about the work they are doing. I know the King in Jordan has been very open and meeting with different religious leaders, both from sort of an Islamic perspective to reduce the lure of the ISIL, but, also, how do we work with the various religious groups?

And Syria was one of the most tolerant countries in the entire Middle East before all this took place. So, it is important, but there are many groups there that we work with. And that is a way to try to reduce the tension that is going on.

Mr. YOHO. But is there a way to hold those areas that you have the refugees in—you know, they are going to school and they are being abused with whatever type of abuse it is. You know, the human trafficking thing is just unconscionable. But gender abuse, we will say that, how do you go about making—you said you are helping those countries deal with that and you are trying to make sure that they are protected, but how do you go about holding that country or that government of that country accountable? If we are in there giving aid, helping out a bad situation, and they are not living up to that standard, what do we do as far as holding those people accountable? Or do we not get into that?

Mr. STAAL. Well, we do in the sense that there are international standards that these countries have signed onto through U.N. Conventions, and so on. And so, that is one advantage, if you will, with working through the U.N. system, is we can hold them accountable for those standards.

Mr. YOHO. Do you feel it is working or is it something that we talk about and, then, we turn a blind eye to it, saying, ''Well, we dealt with it. They are supposed to be doing it,'' but we know it is not getting done? I mean, I have seen that in other parts of the world. I mean, is that what you are seeing over there?

Ms. CLEMENTS. Maybe to give an example of trafficking cases or smuggling cases, or what have you, normally, the aid partners we would work with, if those cases are brought forward, they would work with the local authorities in terms of ensuring followup.

Or, for example, refugees are detained, seeking access, for example, to prisons, to find out whether or not that was a rightful detention or what the due process is for that case to be able to be made. That is part of the protection part of what the organizations do that we support.

I think the broader issue, as Tom has laid out, as part of our dialog, I think, goes well beyond the humanitarian sphere, but obviously connected.

Mr. YOHO. Okay. Then, Mr. Staal, you had brought up that there has been approximately 150 aid workers killed. Does that take into account missing ones? Is there a number of missing people that more than likely could end up as hostages and we will see them on TV one day? And we will regret seeing that. Do you have a sense for how many that are unaccounted for that were aid workers?

Mr. STAAL. Yes. As far as we know right now, there are certainly no Americans held that are unaccounted for that we know of.

Mr. YOHO. Okay.

Mr. STAAL. Most of those 150, frankly, are local Syrians who are working with different organizations that we support.

Mr. YOHO. Okay.

Mr. STAAL. And so, it is that way, yes.

Mr. YOHO. I appreciate your time.

Mr. Chairman, thank you for the extra time, and thank you.

Mr. SMITH. Thank you very much, Mr. Yoho.

Thank you again, Mr. Staal, Ms. Clements, for your tremendous leadership, for providing the two subcommittees with your very fine insights and incisive testimony. It does help us. Of course, by extension, we then brief other Members of Congress. So, thank you.

You are saving lives every single day, and I do think the American public—I have traveled with some DART teams. I remember after the tsunami I was in Sri Lanka. We went from Banda Aceh to Sri Lanka. I was in the van with the DART teams, and I have never been more proud of people who were just absolutely can-do, trying to make the situation better for those who had lost life as well as property during that terrible tsunami.

So, thank you for your leadership.

The hearing is adjourned.

[Whereupon, at 3:38 p.m., the meeting was adjourned.]

APPENDIX

MATERIAL SUBMITTED FOR THE RECORD

JOINT SUBCOMMITTEE HEARING NOTICE
COMMITTEE ON FOREIGN AFFAIRS
U.S. HOUSE OF REPRESENTATIVES
WASHINGTON, DC 20515-6128

Subcommittee on the Middle East and North Africa
Ileana Ros-Lehtinen (R-FL), Chairman

Subcommittee on Africa, Global Health, Global Human Rights, and International Organizations
Christopher H. Smith (R-NJ), Chairman

February 5, 2015

TO: MEMBERS OF THE COMMITTEE ON FOREIGN AFFAIRS

You are respectfully requested to attend an OPEN hearing of the Committee on Foreign Affairs, to be held jointly by the Subcommittee on the Middle East and North Africa, and the Subcommittee on Africa, Global Health, Global Human Rights and International Organizations in Room 2172 of the Rayburn House Office Building (and available live on the Committee website at http://www.ForeignAffairs.house.gov):

DATE: Thursday, February 12, 2015

TIME: 1:30 p.m.

SUBJECT: The Syrian Humanitarian Crisis: Four Years Later and No End in Sight

WITNESSES: Ms. Kelly Tallman Clements
                   Deputy Assistant Secretary
                   Bureau of Population, Refugees, and Migration
                   U.S. Department of State

                   Mr. Thomas Staal
                   Acting Assistant Administrator
                   Bureau for Democracy, Conflict and Humanitarian Assistance
                   U.S. Agency for International Development

By Direction of the Chairman

COMMITTEE ON FOREIGN AFFAIRS

MINUTES OF SUBCOMMITTEE ON _Middle East and North Africa and Africa, Global Human Rights, and International Organizations_ HEARING

Day___*Thursday*___Date_____*2/12/15*_____Room_____*2172*_____

Starting Time ____*1:30 p.m.*___ Ending Time ___*3:38 p.m.*___

Recesses |___*1*___| (*2:15* to *2:43*) (____to ____) (____to ____) (____to ____) (____to ____) (____to ____)

Presiding Member(s)

Chairman Ros-Lehtinen, Chairman Smith

Check all of the following that apply:

Open Session ☑   Electronically Recorded (taped) ☑
Executive (closed) Session ☑   Stenographic Record ☑
Televised ☑

TITLE OF HEARING:

The Syrian Humanitarian Crisis: Four Years Later and No End in Sight

SUBCOMMITTEE MEMBERS PRESENT:

Chairman Ros-Lehtinen, Chairman Smith, Ranking Member Deutch, Reps. Boyle, Chabot, Frankel, and Yoho.

NON-SUBCOMMITTEE MEMBERS PRESENT: *(Mark with an * if they are not members of full committee.)*

None

HEARING WITNESSES: Same as meeting notice attached? Yes ☑ No ☐
(If "no", please list below and include title, agency, department, or organization.)

STATEMENTS FOR THE RECORD: *(List any statements submitted for the record.)*

SFR - Rep. Connolly
SFR - International Rescue Committee

TIME SCHEDULED TO RECONVENE _____
or
TIME ADJOURNED ___*3:38 p.m.*___

Subcommittee Staff Director

Statement for the Record
Submitted by Mr. Connolly of Virginia

The international response to the violence of the Syrian civil war must be multifaceted and include a robust and efficacious humanitarian assistance effort. The scale of the Syrian humanitarian crisis is staggering. It has the potential to profoundly reshape regional demographics and destabilize neighboring countries, which would only spread the violence emanating out of Syria and mire the region in further misery.

After four years, the mass atrocities perpetrated by the regime of President Bashar al-Assad on the Syrian civilian population -- including sectarian violence, mass killings, torture, and the use of chemical weapons and barrel bombs -- show no signs of subsiding. For many Syrians, escaping the reach of the regime risks an encounter with the butchery and oppression of the terrorist organization the Islamic State of Iraq and the Levant (ISIL). It is the ubiquitous violence and destruction of the civil war that has forced nearly 12 million Syrians to flee their homes. There are currently 7.6 million internally displaced persons in Syria and nearly 4 million registered refugees who have fled across Syria's borders.

The proportions of this crisis are a strain on available resources and underline the difficulty local communities and international partners have experienced while attempting to absorb refugee populations and provide adequate humanitarian assistance. In Syria, 53 percent of the population is in need of humanitarian assistance. There are 1.7 million refugees in Lebanon, a country with a population of just 4.5 million, and in Jordan, Syrian refugees amount to 10 percent of the country's population. Turkey has also taken in 1.6 million men, women, and children who left their homes in Syria unsure if they will ever have the opportunity to return.

The international humanitarian response appears to be in triage-mode. Active fighting prevents aid from reaching as many as 5 million people in need, only 20 percent of refugees are housed in camps, and neighboring countries have started to erect barriers to entry to stem the flow of refugees. In the interest of a self-sustaining future for the victims of the Syrian civil war and long-term regional stability we must have a response strategy that extends beyond providing food security, clean water, and preventing the spread of disease. The region simply cannot bear the burden of countries remade by massive populations of individuals who have limited access to education and no opportunity for advancement in their adopted country.

Hopefully, our witnesses can discuss how this response meets immediate needs and contributes to a sustainable future for displaced and affected populations. In carrying out our oversight responsibilities, Chairman Ros-Lehtinen, Ranking Member Deutch, and I have requested a report from the Government Accountability Office regarding the $3 billion the U.S. has allocated for humanitarian operations related to the violence in Syria. It is our intention that this report informs ongoing assistance efforts and aids officials in crafting a humanitarian response that unwinds the deleterious impact the Syrian crisis has had on the region. We cannot allow the legacy of Syria to be a lost generation. To do so would be to perpetuate a cycle of violence, the depths of which we are currently experiencing.

MATERIAL SUBMITTED FOR THE RECORD BY THE HONORABLE ILEANA ROS-LEHTINEN, A REPRESENTATIVE IN CONGRESS FROM THE STATE OF FLORIDA, AND CHAIRMAN, SUBCOMMITTEE ON THE MIDDLE EAST AND NORTH AFRICA

International Rescue Committee
122 East 42ND Street
New York, NY 10168-1289
TEL +1 212 551 3000
FAX +1 212 551 3179

Rescue.org

February 12, 2015

Written Statement for the Record

Submitted by
Sharon Waxman
Vice President for Public Policy and Advocacy
International Rescue Committee

To
The Subcommittee on the Middle East and North
The Subcommittee on Africa, Global Health, and Global Human Rights

For the Joint Subcommittee Hearing
"The Syrian Humanitarian Crisis: Four Years Later and No End in Sight"

The International Rescue Committee (IRC) thanks Chairman Christopher H. Smith, Chairman Ileana Ros-Lehtinen and the subcommittees on the Middle East and North Africa and on Africa, Global Health, and Global Human Rights for holding this hearing. The IRC shares the Committees' deep concern about the safety and security of the Syrian people. IRC has been responding to the needs of the Syrian people and the communities hosting them from since the crisis started nearly 4 years ago.

IRC provides assistance to refugees in Jordan, Lebanon, Turkey, Iraq, and Syria. We provide cash assistance to women in Jordan to minimize their vulnerability to exploitation. Our programs link refugees in Lebanon with potential employers to ease their dependence on international aid. We also supplement local services by providing education to Syrian children and healthcare to Syrian refugees and local communities.

As we approach the 4-year anniversary of the conflict in Syria, more than 12 million are in need of international assistance. More than 7 million people are displaced in Syria, and countries in the region are hosting almost 4 million Syrian refugees.

The humanitarian needs inside Syria are clearly enormous. Today, I would like to bring attention to the plight of Syrian refugees and the needs of countries and communities hosting them across the region.

The countries in the region are under enormous financial and social stress. The World Bank estimates that the cost to the Lebanese economy of hosting Syrian refugees is $7.5 billion. The Government of Turkey estimates the cost to their economy at $4.5 billion. According to IMF and USAID studies about the economic impact on Jordan, there has been a significant drop in the country's annual growth rate, an increase in inflation rates, and loss in tax revenue. In Iraq, 230,000 Syrian refugees have joined more than 2 million already displaced people since January of last year as a result of the recent armed conflict and another 1.1 million who were already displaced by the war Iraq.

The social cost of the conflict is also immense, although it is clearly much harder to quantify. Despite the host counties' welcome to the Syrian people, tensions between host and refugee communities are increasing. There are increasing incidents of curfews being placed on Syrians and evictions from their settlements. Syrians report feeling harassed and exploited.

International Rescue Committee
122 East 42ND Street
New York, NY 10168-1289
TEL +1 212 551 3000
FAX +1 212 551 3179

Rescue.org

IRC thanks the international community, which has provided significant assistance to the region and for having contributed upward of $10 billion since 2012. The United States alone has contributed over $3 billion in life-saving assistance to Syrians in Syria, refugees, and communities hosting them. This money has literally made the difference between life and death for millions of Syrians who have fled the most horrific of circumstances.

Nonetheless, the stress of hosting this massive influx of refugees is leading to a marked deterioration in living conditions for Syrian refugees, and the welcome mat is nearly worn out. To quote a recent report published by the International Rescue Committee and the Norwegian Refugee Council, "The hospitality of countries bordering Syria is at a breaking point."[1]

Syrians are increasingly trapped inside a country where violence continues to deprive them and their families of personal security. The border crossings out of Syria are increasingly closed to those seeking safety. In October 2014, a year that saw high levels of violence in almost all of Syria's governorates, only 18,453 refugees were registered with UNHCR- an 88 percent drop from the 2013 monthly average.

For those seeking refuge in countries neighboring Syria, the ability to live safely and in dignity is diminishing. Refugees have less access to services, particularly in the urban areas of Jordan where 30-50 percent of refugees reside. Jordan has recently changed its health care policy and, as a result, refugees can no longer access free health care services outside camps. This, combined with an increase in evictions, detentions and forcible returns, is making it nearly impossible for refugees to live outside of camps.

The Government of Lebanon has stopped issuing work permits, which prevents refugees from sustaining themselves financially and putting this extremely vulnerable population at greater risk. Due to the high cost of renewing residency permits in Lebanon, refugees face additional challenges as they ravel past checkpoints and are increasingly the targets of raids and evictions. More recently, Lebanon altered its visa requirements for Syrians trying to cross the border. They must have valid passports and meet certain criteria, which can include having minimum amounts of cash on hand and a hotel booking, something impossible for refugees feeling the crisis.

Resettlement to third countries – the only solution for many Syrians and one of the key ways to show solidarity with countries hosting millions of refugees – has been limited to date. Current commitments from the international community are less than 80,000 over a three year period. Thus, less than 2 percent of the registered refugee population has been offered resettlement, and even fewer actually resettled.

In addition to funding international appeals for humanitarian assistance, to mitigate the suffering of civilians, the IRC believes the U.S. Government and its partners in the international community must:

1. Urgently increase its humanitarian and development (including bilateral) support for Lebanon, Jordan, Turkey, and Iraq. Development investments should prioritize improving

---

[1] "No Escape: Civilians in Syria Struggle to Find Safety Across Borders," International Refugee Committee and Norwegian Refugee Council, November 2014. http://www.rescue.org/sites/default/files/resource-file/No%20Escape%20Syria%20report%20IRC%20final%20Nov2014.pdf

International Rescue Committee
122 East 42ND Street
New York, NY 10168-1289
TEL +1 212 551 3000
FAX +1 212 551 3179

Rescue.org

public infrastructure, alternative shelter solutions that increase the overall housing stock, health and education services as well as income-earning opportunities that can best benefit both host communities and refugee populations. If we want these countries to provide refuge, we must give them resources necessary to enable refugees to access local services and restoring the services to pre-crisis levels. At the same time, Lebanon, Turkey, Jordan and Iraq to create a joint appeal to outline the support needed from the international community to ensure that borders are consistently open to civilians fleeing Syria.

2. Ensure that resettlement to third countries increases. Wealthy countries should ensure that at least 5 percent of Syrians – 185,000 refugees -- are resettled swiftly by the end of 2015. The IRC calls on the U.S. to do its fair share and offer resettlement to at least 65,000 Syrian refugees over the next 3 years. This would not be an unprecedented effort. In 2014 alone, the U.S. resettled almost 20,000 Iraqis. To cite another example, since 2006 the U.S. has resettled more than 135,000 Burmese refugees.

3. Seek to firmly implement UNHCR's new policy on alternatives to camps as it pertains to the Middle East. This policy commits UNHCR to pursue alternatives to refugee camps whenever possible and sets out a number of implementation goals. Enabling refugees to earn income and find shelter outside camps should top the priority list.

Thank you for your consideration of our recommendations.

www.ingramcontent.com/pod-product-compliance
Lightning Source LLC
Chambersburg PA
CBHW080907290526

45795CB00007BA/2445